CULTURE BUILDS COMMUNITIES
A Guide to Partnership Building and Putting Culture to Work on Social Issues

Partners for Livable Communities

by

Kathy Booth
Program Officer

with Funding from Citibank

©1995 by Partners for Livable Communities. All rights reserved.
Published 1995.
Printed in the United States of America.

ISBN 0-941182-21-5

Funded by:
Citibank

Illustrations and Book Design by:
Tom Bellucci
1608 Farm Brook Place
Charlottesville, VA 22901

Partners for Livable Communities
1429 21st Street NW
Washington, DC 20036
202/887-5990
202/466-4845 (fax)

About Partners for Livable Communities

Partners for Livable Communities is a nonprofit organization working to improve the livability of communities by promoting quality of life, economic development, and social equity. Since its founding in 1977, Partners has helped communities set a common vision for the future, discover and use new resources for community and economic development, and build public-private coalitions to further their goals. A national resource and information center, Partners generates civic improvements through technical assistance, leadership training, workshops, charettes, research, and publications.

CONTENTS

ACKNOWLEDGMENTS   i

FOREWORD   Paul Ostergard, Vice President, Citibank   iii

INTRODUCTION   Robert H. McNulty, President, Partners for Livable Communities   iv

PROLOGUE — Setting the Stage   1

Redefining the role of cultural resources   3

The broader definition of culture   4

Tackling problems through partnership   4

The chapters to come   5

CHAPTER ONE — Cultural Resources: Critical Tools for Social Agendas   6

Youth advocacy groups   7

Educators   8

Multicultural projects   10

Civil rights organizations   11

Cultural organizations   12

The public sector   13

Community development corporations   15

Beginning the journey   16

CHAPTER TWO — Groundwork: Questions to Ask and Issues to Explore Before Adopting a Strategy   17

Defining your terms   19
    Community   19
    Arts and culture   21

Identifying critical issues in your community   23

Clarifying your vision   25
    Capturing your dreams   25
    The questions of time and energy   28
    Determining your motives   28

Barriers and assets	**30**
Opportunities and strategies	**34**
Finding your partners	**37**
Next steps	**39**

CHAPTER THREE — Collaboration: Strategic Planning and Action Steps   **40**

Prepare internally	**41**
Cultivate potential partners	**41**
Identify a flagship idea	**41**
Set parameters for a plan	**42**
Create a strategic plan	**43**
Formulate an organizational structure	**44**
The advisory body	**44**
The implementing team	**45**
Solidify funding	**45**
A note on process	**46**

CHAPTER FOUR — Troubleshooting: The Nature of Partnerships   **47**

Developing a common plan	**48**
The limits of compromise	**50**
Taking time to build a project	**50**
Translating across working styles	**50**
Building trust	**52**
Attention to process	**53**
Why some partnerships fail	**56**
Distrusting each others' motives	**56**
An unequal balance of power	**56**
An inappropriate division of roles	**58**
From process to action	**59**

CHAPTER FIVE — Action: Carrying Out Your Plan	60
Launching an initial program	61
Various models of assessment and documentation	62
Recording participation	62
Questionnaires	63
Recording the process	63
Combating social problems	65
Using assessment methods from other fields	66
Formal evaluations	67
Sustaining your vision	67
An institutionalized approach to leadership	67
Continue building support	69
Marking the Beginning	69
CONCLUSION	70
APPENDIX A — Partners for Livable Communities: A Partner in Action	72
APPENDIX B — Further Resources for Cultural Community Collaborations	74
INDEX OF BEST PRACTICES	82

ACKNOWLEDGMENTS

Partners for Livable Communities' work on *Culture Builds Communities* was made possible and greatly enhanced by the input of many distinguished individuals and organizations.

The need for this book was first voiced at a national leadership forum held at the Smithsonian Institution in Washington, D.C. in December 1994. The "Culture Builds Communities" forum drew 170 participants from around the country representing the public sector, funders, arts and cultural institutions, youth and civil rights advocacy groups, and community-based organizations. Together, they explored how cultural institutions and communities can join forces to address issues of multicultural understanding and equal opportunity, community empowerment, and youth and families. Our gratitude goes to all those practitioners and advocates who first inspired this writing, and to the National Endowment for the Arts, which funded the conference.

Partners is particularly indebted to Citibank, which provided a matching grant for the Smithsonian forum and funding for this document. Special thanks goes to Brandee Galvin, Assistant Vice President, who has consistently offered support and critique to the full range of Partners' work.

Partners owes the success of the Smithsonian forum to the advising and recruiting efforts of our conference co-sponsors:

American Council for the Arts
  (New York, NY)
International City/County
  Management Association
  (Washington, DC)
President's Committee on the Arts
  and the Humanities
  (Washington, DC)
Smithsonian Institution
  (Washington, DC)

Partners has been further aided in our work on "Culture Builds Communities" issues by a national advisory committee. These knowledgeable individuals have helped Partners' work stay grounded in a broad spectrum of communities and disciplines:

Luis Cancel, President, American Council
  for the Arts (New York, NY)
Tom Freudenheim, Assistant Provost for
  the Arts and Humanities, Smithsonian
  Institution (Washington, DC)
William Hansell, Executive Director,
  International City/County
  Management Association
  (Washington, DC)
William Strickland, Executive Director,
  Manchester Craftsman's Guild
  (Pittsburgh, PA)
Ruby Takanishi, Executive Director,
  Carnegie Council on Adolescent
  Development (Washington, DC)
Raul Yzaguirre, President, National
  Council of La Raza (Washington, DC)

This book would not have been possible without the generous amounts of information offered by people doing this work all over the country. Partners would like to extend great thanks to:

Barbara Anderson, Forsyth County
  Library (Winson-Salem, NC)
Judy Baca, Social and Public Art Resource
  Center (Venice, CA)
Matthew Bauer, New York Main Street
  Alliance (Staten Island, NY)
Frank Blechman, George Mason
  University Conflict Analysis
  Resolution Center (Fairfax, VA)

Nancy Brennan, Baltimore City Life Museums (Baltimore, MD)
Dee Covington, Break the Cycle Teen Theatre Troupe (Longmont, CO)
Eve Diaz, Guadalupe Cultural Arts Center (San Antonio, TX)
Steve Davies, Project for Public Spaces (New York, NY)
Luz de la Riva, Sangre Latina (Richmond, CA)
Ray Doughty, Arts in the Basic Curriculum (Rock Hill, SC)
Meg Fagin, Gowanus Arts Exchange (New York, NY)
Ryan Gilliam, Downtown Art Co. (New York, NY)
Portia Hamilton-Sperr, The Philadelphia Initiative for Cultural Pluralism (Philadelphia, PA)
Mary Ruffin Hanbury, Portsmouth Community Development Group (Portsmouth, VA)
Pat Jacobs-MacDonald, Black Economic Union of Greater Kansas City (Kansas City, MO)
Bobbie Johnson, Race to Knowledge (Chicago, IL)
Carmen James Lane, Humanities Council of Washington, DC (Washington, DC)
Aleta Margolis, Adjunct Professor, American University School of Education (Washington, DC)
Harvey Milkman, Project SelfDiscovery (Denver, CO)
Gustavo Paredes, Northwestern University Settlement Association (Chicago, IL)
Cynthia Peters, Parks, Recreation and Library Department (Phoenix, AZ)
Carol Clarke Sampson, Cultural Arts Program of the City of Dayton, OH (Dayton, OH)
Shane Smith, Cheyenne Botanic Garden (Cheyenne, WY)
Karen Trella, Neighborhood Housing Services (New York, NY)
Jill Warzer, South Carolina Arts Commission (Columbia, SC)
Laura Jean Watters, Council on the Arts and Humanities for Staten Island (Staten Island, NY)
Patryc Wiggins, Mill Tapestry Project (Newport, NH)

Partners also wishes to thank the following organizations, where we spoke to many staff members:
Artists Collective (Hartford, CT)
Artspace Projects, Inc. (Minneapolis, MN)
Bend in the River (Dubuque, IA)
Bronx Council on the Arts (New York, NY)
Cultural Collaborative Jamaica (New York, NY)
Living Stage Theatre Company (Washington, DC)
Manchester Craftsman's Guild (Pittsburgh, PA)
Learning Through Education and Arts Partnerships (West Palm Beach, FL)
Three Rivers Arts Festival (Pittsburgh, PA)

Partners is deeply thankful to our editors and readers, whose incisive comments helped this book take its final form:
Jeff Gibney, Executive Director, South Bend Heritage Foundation (South Bend, IN)
Jim Kunde, Executive Director, Coalition to Improve Management in State and Local Government (Arlington, TX)
Kathleen Murnion, Program Consultant, Brooklyn In Touch (New York, NY)
Clint Page, Senior Associate, Partners for Livable Communities (Washington, DC)
Mat Schwarzman, Project Director, Urban Arts Institute (Oakland, CA)

Finally, the depth of this work was made possible by a grant from the Rockefeller Foundation that enabled Partners to document how artist activists use culture to build communities. Many thanks!

ACKNOWLEDGMENTS

FOREWORD

As a global company with a unique worldwide presence, Citibank is an important partner in the business and civic life of the cities and countries where we do business. We believe that our commitment to good citizenship includes investment in programs that contribute to economic vitality, community development, and the attainment of human potential. Fulfilling our responsibility to communities is not only the right thing to do — it is good business.

We meet the needs of the communities we serve around the world through our business activities and extensive philanthropic work. As in our businesses, we practice success transfer, adapting ideas and techniques that work in one community to others around the globe. *Culture Builds Communities* is a good example.

Across our markets we have seen the positive role that arts and culture have played in neighborhood revitalization. The arts are essential not only in improving overall quality of life, but in strengthening business and housing development. It is our hope that this manual will enable you to take strategies that have proven successful in one community and adapt them to your own.

We are grateful to Partners for Livable Communities for producing this publication and look forward to learning about new "Culture Builds Communities" successes.

Paul Ostergard
Vice President and Director of
Corporate Contributions,
Citibank

INTRODUCTION

Culture Builds Communities is a great resource for citizen and civic leaders who are dealing with these pressing problems of our cities:

- youth at risk, youth development, mentoring

- economic development, economic opportunity, preparation for labor force

- equal rights, multiculturalism, race relations, equality, and fairness

- community development, community-based strategies, neighborhood revitalization

- public accountability and entrepreneurial management

This book contains strategies by which your interests, central to the future of any community, can be teamed with arts and cultural resources to aid community problem solving. We are in a time not only of economic crisis, but of transition from one era to another; one in which there are "global transfers of moneys, goods, technology, and information," to quote Gerard Paquet, a French cultural organizer. "People are baffled and confused, and what they need is a political and cultural response that gives them the hope of a better world," or in our definition, a better community. Partners believes that culture is not only a problem solver and a resource, but a glue to mend the shredding fabric of our communities.

Partners wishes to give special thanks to Citibank through the New York-area program, "Culture Builds Community," and for the sponsorship, not only of the forum at the Smithsonian, but for this publication.

There are three scales that I hope you will consider as you read this book and picture how it may aid you:

1) Individual institutions — such as libraries, museums, performing arts centers, community-based cultural groups — in partnership with social, economic, or human development concerns, can become fulcrums of change. By redefining their identities around solving community problems, these institutions can expand their importance in the life of the community.

2) Partnerships can spring up between a number of community development institutions and cultural resources to implement social strategies. Programs such as the Community Foundation for Youth Initiatives explore how institutions can become direct service providers in supporting the agenda and goals of social, economic, or community action.

3) An entire community can examine its cultural resources to see how these resources can be woven together into a support structure for the central needs of the community.

This publication is not only a guide, but a challenge. Could you put culture to work in building your community? Good thinking!

Robert H. McNulty
President
Partners for Livable Communities

PROLOGUE
SETTING THE STAGE

In the United States, we learn from the first days of school that this nation is built on freedom. We are taught that our economy is based on entrepreneurship and that everyone has the power to make something of themselves. Yet, many of today's children — and many adults — lack the basic skills, economic opportunities, and connections to a community that are necessary to succeed. Moreover, many people do not truly believe that they have the power to shape and change their lives. When people lose the power to imagine new possibilities and the routes to get there, our nation begins to lose its inherent potential. All of our efforts to ensure a decent quality of life, whether through policy reforms, community development, or human services, will fail if people are not capable of action.

The South Bend Heritage Foundation (SBHF), a community development corporation in South Bend, Indiana, has found one way both to get people dreaming and to give them the skills to achieve those dreams. Residents of South Bend's Near West Side, a predominantly African-American neighborhood, suffer from a 16.8 percent unemployment rate and half the average family income of the surrounding county. When nearby schools and recreational institutions were abandoned, young people were left with a dim sense of their future and dangerously little to do. The SBHF's Colfax Cultural Center Complex helps fill some of those gaps.

With two decades experience in overcoming urban blight and revitalizing inner city neighborhoods, SBHF recognizes the critical role that a vibrant community center — offering a range of service, entertainment, and skills building options — can play in sustaining and improving low-income areas. That is why the organization founded the Colfax Cultural Center in 1983. Today, the

Complex is home to low-cost art studios, classrooms, performance spaces, and twenty-two nonprofit offices, including several small businesses and fifteen social service agencies. An adjacent building, the Charles Martin Annex, houses a multipurpose youth center, with a special emphasis on minority and inner-city youths.

At the two facilities, social service providers screen children for developmental delays, offer self-esteem programs, and run a day care center. Tenants such as the Girl Scouts, the South Bend Regional Museum of Art, and the Indiana University Division of Arts help Near West Side residents imagine and portray new possibilities for their lives through professional performances and training in dance, theater, and music. College-preparatory agencies train students in the skills necessary to succeed. And, the facility has created a natural gathering place for the community to hold festivals and performances — activities that make the neighborhood more attractive to potential investors. Because of its focus on both the arts and community, SBHF has been able to attract an unusual mix of tenants and programs, thereby creating a more seamless web of intervention, services, and skills building.

All across the country, through programs like the Colfax Cultural Center Complex, community leaders, activists, and the public sector are discovering that their efforts to tackle social problems are enhanced by using arts and cultural resources. This book provides the skills to employ arts and cultural resources for the task of helping people achieve their potential. Aimed at concerns such as community development, youth at risk, civil rights, and neighborhood empowerment, *Culture Builds Communities* walks through the process of building partnerships between socially and culturally oriented organizations.

REDEFINING THE ROLE OF CULTURAL RESOURCES

Arts and cultural resources have much to offer individuals and communities to foster understanding, skills building, and rejuvenation. They address basics such as self-esteem and the power to influence one's surroundings. They can be used to alter the image of an area, express anger and fear, provide a common meeting ground, and create safe havens from dangerous settings. Arts and cultural programs stimulate economic growth, create jobs, and build job skills. And because they define who we are in all of our diversity, they are central in binding and mending the social fabric of our communities.

Despite the possibilities that arts and cultural resources have to offer, these programs are the first to face cuts when budgets get tight or crises arise. Given the pressing economic and social needs and eroding physical infrastructures that plague our communities, decision makers must choose how to allocate scarce resources among competing and worthwhile objectives. Many feel that they cannot justify spending on activities that fall into the seemingly elitist or less crucial categories of arts and culture. Unfortunately, this misperception can obscure how art and culture can be powerful problem solving tools.

Arts and culture need to be redefined, not as frills or luxuries, but as essential and useful agents for invigorating and restoring character to our communities. When used in tandem with more conventional problem solving tactics, arts and culture can become significant vehicles for building leadership, communication, and participation. Arts and culture are effective because they help address some of the less cut-and-dried issues that nonetheless color our ability to attack the causes of intolerance, community deterioration, youth at risk, and other social concerns.

Cultural community programs can take a number of forms, including:

Community arts centers

Educational or community-building theater

Festivals

Anti-racism and tolerance-building projects

Youth at risk intervention programs

Community rehabilitation projects through physical design

Historic preservation and tourism

School curricula that use the arts to teach other subjects

PROLOGUE

THE BROADER DEFINITION OF CULTURE

Part of redefining the role that arts and culture can play is reexamining how we envision them in the first place. When many people think of art, they think of specific performing arts, such as opera or the theater, or visual arts like paintings and sculptures. Similarly, culture can be seen as high art — the complex and sometimes inaccessible representation of ideas. Neither of these definitions, however, scratches the surface of the rich arts and cultural traditions that exist and intertwine in the United States.

"Culture"
Webster's New Collegiate Dictionary

1) Cultivation, tillage

2) The act of developing the intellectual and moral faculties, especially by education

3) Expert care and training

4b) Acquaintance with and taste in fine arts, humanities, and broad aspects of science...

5a) The integrated pattern of human behavior that includes thought, speech, action, and artifacts and depends upon man's capacity for learning and transmitting knowledge to succeeding generations

5b) The customary beliefs, social forms, and material traits of a racial, religious, or social group

For the purpose of this work, "culture" is defined as creative expressions of identity, place, and meaning; it encompasses both the arts and humanities. There are a host of cultural institutions: traditional ones such as art museums and theaters, but also science museums, parks and recreation programs, community-based arts centers, ethnically focused community centers, zoos, botanical gardens, and libraries. In addition to painting and sculpture, culture can be found in neighborhood murals, music, festivals, and in landscaped parks that celebrate the heritage of an area. Culture, in this context, is active and participatory, as opposed to more passive appreciation.

Once we begin to see cultural resources through a larger lens, a host of opportunities arise. Under this new definition, many community development and advocacy organizations discover that they are already using cultural resources, and arts organizations realize that they have more allies than they may have originally believed.

Coming to see the role that culture can play is the first step in innovative community problem solving. In order to achieve results, however, this new perception must be put into action, and cultural resources need to be woven into standard tactics.

Engaging in community problem solving from a single institutional point of view has some disadvantages. Because there are so many factors shaping our society's problems, no one approach is likely to hold the key, and different organizations have different strengths and reach different constituencies. Given the scarcity of resources available to both cultural insti-

TACKLING PROBLEMS THROUGH PARTNERSHIPS

PROLOGUE

tutions and those working on community issues, working together can bring significant advantages. Coordination prevents duplication, widens the resource base, and infuses each partner's work with new perceptions. In agriculture, hybrids often yield the strongest and most resilient results. *Similarly, cultural resources teamed with a social or public service focus provide creative, innovative perspectives that can help more traditional programs grow to new heights of effectiveness.* Even within organizations, taking on this multiple approach can open new realms of innovation. In single institution projects, the larger community can become a partner in action.

THE CHAPTERS TO COME

This manual will enhance community stakeholders' and motivated individuals' efforts to address pressing community concerns by giving an honest, thorough look at what cultural community partnerships can offer and what it will take to create them. The chapters that follow begin by telling the stories of people who have taken the initiative to make a difference in their communities. The descriptions of their projects form a base for the later chapters, which will employ your stories, hopes, and concerns to determine the best route to a productive cultural community partnership.

Each chapter is designed to stand on its own and covers issues from a comprehensive standpoint in order to accommodate the various perspectives that this manual is designed for. Pick and choose chapters and subsections as they are useful and relevant to your experience in this arena. This book is also intended to be interactive. There are many questions to help frame a developing project and space in the margins to write comments. It can be used to help articulate an individual vision, with a board to facilitate the evolution of the project, or with the actual institutions that are creating a partnership.

Who This Book Is For

- Community development corporations
- Community cultural centers
- Neighborhood organizations
- Libraries
- Civil rights organizations
- Parks departments
- Performing arts centers
- Youth advocacy organizations
- Zoos
- Public officials
- Botanical gardens
- Museums

Using culture as a critical tool in social agendas means daring to explore beyond the boundaries of existing definitions and organizational lines to rediscover the cultural resources that already root us in society. This book, with its wealth of case studies and frank assessments of resources, will ease you through this process and lay the groundwork for a durable and well-focused project.

PROLOGUE

CHAPTER ONE
CULTURAL RESOURCES:
CRITICAL TOOLS FOR SOCIAL AGENDAS

Although culture may not be perceived as a bread-and-butter issue — and thus given little credibility, energy, or funding — it is a valuable agent for confronting many troubling social issues. Cultural resources, found in libraries, museums, zoos, parks, local cultural centers, and visual and performing arts centers, and used by individual artists, can be readily employed by a wide range of professional fields both to enhance their abilities to solve problems creatively and to reach troubled populations. Cultural facilities are often centrally located and may be natural meeting places, like the library or a community arts center. Further, many cultural facilities are actively engaged in the community or are seeking new ways to strengthen their involvement in social issues. But most important, working at the intersection of culture and community can yield new, more effective and holistic approaches to community development.

Because "culture" is defined so broadly, there are many ways that it can be put to work on social agendas. This chapter presents seven examples of how cultural resources are being marshaled by different professional fields, at various levels of collaborative complexity, with a range of budgets. They will provide a host of ideas for projects and unveil new partnership possibilities.

YOUTH ADVOCACY GROUPS

Among the multitude of troubling issues that face our society, the plight of youth is a constant theme. Not only are children more likely to live at or below the poverty level, today's youths face increasing pressure to engage in destructive behavior at earlier and earlier ages. Seventy-seven percent of eighth graders report having used alcohol; 30 percent of young adolescents report having had sexual intercourse by age fifteen; and suicide rates have increased 75 percent among ten to fourteen-year-olds between 1979 and 1988 (statistics drawn from report by the Carnegie Council on Adolescent Development, 1994, **see Appendix B** for more information). The prevalence of gangs and the accompanying drug use and violence are also a serious threat, not only in the inner city, but in suburban and rural areas as well.

Many youth workers have discovered that cultural resources can be used to simultaneously provide alternative activities for young people; warn them of the consequences of activities like drinking, pregnancy, and dropping out; and equip them with basic life skills. The characteristics of culture — the use of creativity, its ability to carry messages, the way it gives form to values and perceptions — make it a tool that young people use readily. In many ways cultural activities are a natural extension of playing, something that even the most jaded adolescent knows how to do. Therefore, cultural programs are springing up everywhere to offer new opportunities to troubled young people.

Break the Cycle
Teen Theatre Troupe

Longmont, Colorado

Troubled youths perform self-written plays and provide peer counseling for other young people.

"Break the Cycle" Teen Theatre Troupe uses theater arts as a prevention strategy by delivering powerful messages to teens about family violence, teen pregnancy, substance abuse, environmental issues,

> "Children who pick up a paintbrush or a pen, a clarinet or a fistful of clay are less likely to pick up a needle or a gun. They've got better things to do."
>
> —*Jane Alexander,
> Chair, National Endowment for the Arts*

and understanding diversity. The troupe, made up of troubled youths, has performed at schools, churches, shelters, civic and service clubs, and other community settings. It has also been recognized nationally and has performed at several national conferences.

To engage the troupe members on all levels, and thus to give them an opportunity to become role models rather than troublemakers, performances are designed by the students themselves. After each presentation, troupe members lead in discussing the tough issues that they have raised. With the benefit of 200 hours of peer counselor training, "Break the Cycle" actors also work one-on-one with people after these discussions.

"Break the Cycle" was developed by the Network for Youth Empowerment, a partnership to address Longmont's high teen pregnancy rate. The Network is made up of city and county departments, school districts, pregnancy and adoption services, church groups, and youth disability and women's advocacy centers. Despite

CHAPTER ONE

widely different views on specifics such as birth control, abortion, and sex education, all found common ground in the use of theater as an intervention tool. The City's Division of Youth Services was chosen to lead the program, with support from the local arts council and other cultural organizations. Funding has been drawn from a wide range of sources, including the United Way, the Division of Youth Service, schools, honoraria, service clubs, private contributions, and even T-shirt sales.

Research shows that prevention messages are most effective when combined with an impact on the emotions, and for teens, when presented by their peers. "Break the Cycle's" performances bear this out by eliciting powerful responses from audience members, both in discussions and in post-performance evaluations. Their most obvious effect, however, is in the lives of the troupe members. Through their commitment to a four-times-weekly rehearsal schedule and their new leadership role, these teens not only affect the life decisions of others, they are given the chance to turn around their own.

EDUCATORS

Cultural programs are not only effective for crisis intervention — they are excellent tools to facilitate education in general. Arts-based curricula, because they are interactive rather than passive, help develop critical thinking skills and build the capacity to organize, recast, and use information to solve problems. Arts-based curricula also reach students who do poorly with traditional education models, because some people learn better through hands-on activities rather than through reading and writing.

Project Zero, a division of the Harvard School of Education, has generated a number of studies on the role of the arts in education. One of the conclusions of this research is that there are many ways that people solve problems, known as "multiple intelligences." Given that most schools value learning styles that use language, logic, and math skills, those who learn best using movement or through working with others are at a disadvantage. If given the opportunity to process

> "We are no longer a manufacturing-based economy. The skills needed for the 21st century can be learned through the arts — teamwork, creativity, innovation, being open to change."
>
> — Barbara S. Nielsen,
> South Carolina State Superintendent of Education

information through a different format — such as modeling clay to understand the mathematical concept of surface area — otherwise poor students may suddenly improve their performance on and their understanding of traditional school subjects (**see Appendix B** for more information on Project Zero and this model).

Even basic training in the arts can help students boost their performance. According to the National Arts Education Research Center at New York University, students who study sculpture improve their understanding of geometry. Science, math, and reading scores go up when students study the arts. *Dropout rates, test scores, and the ability to reach poverty-stricken youths are also improved when arts are integrated into school curricula* (**see Appendix B** for more information on these studies and the National Arts Education Research Center).

CHAPTER ONE

Arts in the Basic Curriculum Project/ Target 2000 Arts in Education Grant Program

South Carolina

A school reform package including curriculum frameworks, funding, and public relations boosting perception of the arts as essential to education.

The Arts Based Curriculum Project (ABC) is a South Carolina model program designed to show how quality, comprehensive arts education programs can be designed for every child, using curriculum guidelines in dance, drama, music, and visual arts. This blueprint was created for the state by a steering committee of educators, artists, civic and legislative leaders, cultural and educational institutions, and educational and arts associations, under the leadership of the South Carolina Arts Commission and the South Carolina Department of Education. Although the planning phase was funded by a National Endowment for the Arts grant, project implementation has been made possible through state funding, under legislation that funneled $6.2 million to arts education over five years.

ABC sites may choose to strengthen arts programming or restructure an entire curriculum by making art integral to everyday studies. One site, Redcliffe Elementary School, adopted an arts-infusion approach. For example, teachers have students act out the process of photosynthesis in science class or grasp grammar by dancing their interpretation of action verbs modified by adverbs. Since the program was introduced, test scores have risen dramatically. Top quartile scoring for fourth graders in the Stanford 8 achievement test went from 19 to 33 percent, while the lowest quartile fell from 33 percent to 9 percent.

The collaboration between educators, arts experts, and public officials also generated Target 2000, a grant program that aims to boost creativity and critical thinking by pouring $1 million annually into school arts programs. These funds are used by each district to tailor programs to its specific needs and concerns. The Wil Lou Gray Opportunity School has used Target 2000 funds to boost their work with at-risk students, who are particularly responsive to creative, hands-on activities. The "Arts Afire" program, which focuses on building skills in the arts, has also led to progress in other subjects. The discipline and interest bred by involvement in the arts often help focus otherwise-troubled students and identify their strengths. Teachers at Wil Lou Gray credit "Arts Afire" as a major force in helping students pass the state's exit examination in reading and writing.

State funding has been complemented by an intensive public relations campaign to strengthen other sources of support. The South Carolina Arts Commission encourages business and corporate contributions for arts education under the theme, "In South Carolina, Arts Education Means Business." This includes television public service announcements, brochures, informational posters, and bumper stickers. Educators and administrators will also anchor support with data documenting the concrete effects of the ABC Project and Target 2000. This information will be collected over the next two years under the guidance of the ABC Project. Nevertheless, the most compelling testimony comes from the lives of the students themselves, who are using the arts to springboard into the twenty-first century, armed with the skills necessary for success.

CHAPTER ONE

MULTICULTURAL PROJECTS

In addition to educating people in school, cultural resources are excellent tools to increase understanding between ethnic communities. Cultural traditions preserve who we are, were, and hope to be, and present that information in tangible form. They also provide an entry point for exchange between groups. Works of art express the artist's fundamental human condition, and therefore can show the common bonds that unite us. It is far less threatening to sample food, watch dance, and listen to stories than it is to discuss deep tensions between immigrant and more established communities. If these activities are thoughtfully paired with opportunities to explore deeper issues, they can be an extremely effective way to bring a broad array of people to the table. *Once people better understand the reference points of other cultures and find common values, they are more likely to be open to other ways of life.* For this reason, cultural resources such as festivals are an excellent medium with which to address explosive examples of racism in a community.

Bend in the River

Dubuque, Iowa

A festival to address racism, including both diversity training and multicultural food, music, and art exchange.

In the aftermath of cross-burnings in the yards of several African-Americans, residents of Dubuque, Iowa, rallied to educate themselves through an annual multicultural human relations conference. After three years, however, it became apparent that those who attended the conferences did not represent the ethnic, religious, generational, or economic diversity of the area. In order to increase community participation, the conference was coupled with an international festival, with the arts used as a lure to start discussions about community problems.

The two-day event, dubbed "Bend in the River," was designed by a steering committee made up of a broad cross-section of people representing education, government, labor, arts, business, student, religious, social service, law, and human rights agencies. Funding was secured through the state arts council, the humanities board, a community cultural grant program, public sector support, US West, and local businesses and individuals.

The festival featured a series of diversity seminars — some directed specifically toward businesses, others to the general public — covering mediation training, abuse, and cross-cultural relations. The conference also convened simultaneous town meetings to elicit community concerns, questions, and recommendations for action. Recommendations were printed immediately after these meetings and then directed toward specific organizations within the city. Throughout the weekend, cultural activities like exhibits, plays, global bazaars, and dances were also set up to engage people from different backgrounds with each other more directly.

CHAPTER ONE

"Bend in the River" successfully allowed a broad cross-section of the community to identify joint goals and action steps to support diversity awareness and strengthen the community. This helped to keep community projects on track and exposed the people of Dubuque to the wealth of traditions already thriving side-by-side.

CIVIL RIGHTS ORGANIZATIONS

Festivals offer an opportunity to celebrate cultural traditions and highlight their value for a set period of time. However, these traditions are meaningful because of their place in daily life. Early in the civil rights movement, many organizations included a strong cultural component, which strove to educate people about their heritage. Today, however, most civil rights organizations (or the advocacy and skills-building organizations that they generated) have little or no staff to support a cultural agenda, seldom sponsor cultural programming, and rarely include culture as an element of their national conferences or training programs. In part, this is because intensive work has been focused on basic needs, like expanding job opportunities or providing housing.

However, one of the resources that communities of color have to draw on — and which needs to be actively celebrated and preserved — is cultural heritage. Traditional dances, songs, stories, and images can help rebuild a sense of identity and worth in young people and ground them in history. Infusing people with an understanding of their culture does not need to replace work done on basic needs. In fact, a cultural approach can be integral to basic concerns. Low-income housing doesn't have to stop with a roof and four walls; it should include space for people to meet and tell stories and to display who they are. Cultural elements not only infuse the struggle for survival with beauty, they can facilitate pride and connectedness to one's place.

City Lights

Washington, DC

A cultural history project that brings storytellers and artists from various ethnic traditions into public housing and provides funds for heritage projects.

Many public housing communities occupied by people of color have discovered that intergenerational cultural projects, such as collecting oral histories and then creating displays to tell these stories, are an excellent way to build trust, community, and a sense of safety. For example, Potomac Gardens, a public housing site near the U.S. Capitol in Washington, DC, employed this approach through a project called City Lights. Run by the Humanities Council of Washington, DC, City Lights brings scholars, storytellers, and performers to public housing sites to highlight African-American history and heritage for both youth and adult audiences. In addition to presenting, these facilitators encourage residents to share their own stories. The Humanities Council, with support from the National Endowment for the Humanities, also awards grants to local community groups for public humanities programs.

After several City Lights programs, Potomac Gardens residents began to share their life stories with each other and discovered that there were many common threads. With the encourage-

> "Museums can serve to bring diverse points of view together in a dialogue. They can allow for a free flow of information and opinions, and they can be a place from which new information and ideas emerge."
>
> — Patricia Williams,
> Deputy Director of Programs and Policy,
> American Association of Museums

CHAPTER ONE

ment and assistance of the Humanities Council, residents applied for a grant to create "In Search of Common Ground," a heritage survey on birthplaces, migration patterns, first jobs, and families. The survey culminated in a "Down Home Week," with each day being dedicated to a different birthplace or region, and seniors sharing memorabilia and stories. The program was such a success that Potomac Gardens residents applied for a second grant to do a full oral history project. Local scholars and the Historical Society were brought in to train residents on how to gather oral histories. In 1994, the project culminated in a thirteen minute video — which has received awards from film and humanities competitions — and an exhibit at the Smithsonian's Anacostia Museum.

In addition to the friendships built and skills learned, City Lights has had a profound impact on the residents of public housing sites. In the words of Thelma Russell, president of the Potomac Gardens Senior Resident Council,

"The fact that City Lights has come and stayed in our community has enabled residents to trust the program, especially when so many services in public housing come and go easily....These programs have helped us listen to one another and to learn from each other. The education most of us received taught us that Black people did not exist, let alone contribute anything worthwhile to our city and our nation. City Lights is filling in the gaps and showing us that we are a part of history....We were strangers before; now we understand that our common ground is the African-American heritage that we share."

CULTURAL ORGANIZATIONS

Our collective heritages are most clearly documented through cultural institutions and organizations. Although some facilities draw their value from showcasing specific aesthetic forms, many are beginning to take more active roles in society. Some are facing public demands that they become more accessible or have found that they need to cultivate new audiences. Others are realizing that their missions lead logically to involvement in social issues.

In 1984, the American Association of Museums challenged America's museums to look seriously at the forces shaping their future: increasing public participation in decisionmaking; the acceptance of the importance of lifelong learning; the shift to an economy based on creating and transferring information; and the growing recognition of our society's pluralistic nature. More than a decade later, these forces are even more evident. *Whether they are botanical gardens, science museums, libraries, or even community cultural centers, cultural institutions are increasingly taking leadership roles in America's social agendas.*

Guadalupe Cultural Arts Center

San Antonio, Texas

The foremost Latino multidisciplinary cultural center in the country, promoting economic development among the Latino population.

Located in a Mexican-American neighborhood that has the eleventh lowest per capital income in the country, the Guadalupe Cultural Arts Center (GCAC) offers an outstanding example of how cultural institutions can cultivate a healthy economy. GCAC is a nonprofit, multidisciplinary arts organization dedicated to the preservation, development, and promotion of Mexican-American arts and to facilitating a deeper understanding and appreciation of Chicano/Latino and Native American cultures. Toward these ends, the organization offers programs and classes in Chicano art history, music, literature, visual arts, theater, dance, and media. The Historic Guadalupe Theater includes a visual arts gallery and spaces for performing, film, and video events — from traditional music festivals to competitions featuring international Latino films. Other annual events include a book fair, a literary reading series, a season of plays by the resident acting company, a concert series, and a fine arts and crafts market.

GCAC has a budget of nearly $1.5 million; one-third of the revenue is earned, with other support coming from the public sector, the National Endowment for the Arts, foundations, and businesses like Target Stores and Anheuser-Busch. Overall, the organization's audiences number 100,000 people a year from broad ethnic, economic, and geographic backgrounds.

By offering a sophisticated venue for Latino art and culture, GCAC already plays a significant role in addressing community issues in San Antonio, where more than half the population is Chicano. But the organization does more than simply showcase cultural traditions and expressions. It also strives to make an economic impact.

First, GCAC provides jobs for Chicano artists and arts administrators. It has a permanent, full-time staff of eighteen and provides short-term employment or exhibition opportunities to more than 400 individual artists, writers, actors, and performers, and about fifty music, dance, and theater groups yearly. Second, GCAC has spawned other Hispanic-focused organizations and businesses. The Avenida Guadalupe Association, an economic development group that incubates Chicano business, renovated a marketplace across from GCAC. By first creating amenities and basic services in this low-income area, the Association is erecting the infrastructure to enable a higher standard of living for residents in the poorest of neighborhoods.

The public sector has an important role to play in cultural partnerships. Elected and appointed officials, by nature of their ability to allocate financial support and to supervise management, can contribute to both cultural and social issues. Many of the community's natural gathering places are public facilities — such as parks, schools, and libraries. *Through creative programming, basic resources such as these can become popular destinations for youths, and thus become a way to easily identify and channel high-risk youths into intervention programming.*

Public officials have expressed their support for cultural strategies through a number of avenues. The International City/County Management Association has featured strategic cultural plans at its annual meetings and in its publications, and the U.S. Conference of Mayors has adopted several policy resolutions on the value of arts and culture. In addition, local and state arts agencies, which are often funded publicly, offer a natural bridge between the two realms and often can be found in the crux of cultural and community work.

THE PUBLIC SECTOR

CHAPTER ONE

Phoenix Parks, Recreation and Library Department

Phoenix, Arizona

A recreation program offering employment, life, and remedial skills in community centers and from mobile recreation units.

Since 1980, the South Phoenix Youth Center, a division of the Parks, Recreation and Library Department, has been a focal point for promoting positive teen development among at-risk youth. The center has three primary services: recreation, employment, and prevention. Typically, youths are attracted to the center because of recreation programs such as swim parties and talent shows. Once students are drawn to the center and its safe, nonthreatening environment, however, they often enter job and intervention programs such as the Teens 'N' Training Program (TNT) and the Teen Education Enrichment Network (TEEN) Program.

The TNT program is a complete education, career training, counseling, and support program for fourteen to twenty-one-year-olds, partially funded through the Jobs Training Partnership Act. In addition to providing classes on topics such as communication and remedial skills, the program also funnels youths into GED and vocational training and offers a bi-annual job fair. More than 1,500 youths receive information through the TNT program each year.

The TEEN program, funded partially through a grant from a community foundation, aims to provide activities for high-risk youths to prevent destructive behavior like drug abuse, gang activity, and teen pregnancy. Support groups, educational presentations, and information fairs build self-esteem and resiliency, sharpen critical life skills, and give these young people positive peer support.

The Parks, Recreation and Library Department also runs mobile programs late at night and on weekends. City Streets, which serves high-risk neighborhoods that do not have access to parks, offers individual counseling and referrals, in addition to foos-ball, ping-pong, books, a sound system, and computers to teach math and science skills. In 1990, while still in its pilot stage, City Streets was cited by the Carnegie Council on Adolescent Development as one of the ten best youth programs in the nation. Since then, City Streets has been expanded to serve the entire city.

The Department has also expanded its programming as a whole. Since 1993, a new Youth At Risk Division has supervised the two city youth centers, the mobile programs, and a host of other youth-related projects. The division serves as a point of connection between youths, other city departments, governmental agencies, schools, and community organizations. It also supervises collaborative projects — for example, two aspects of the City Streets program are run in conjunction with community partners. The City Streets Recreation Internship Program was created with six youth organizations, and the Mobile Partnership Program is run with assistance from local businesses.

All of these programs are further informed by the Teen Parks and Recreation Board and numerous youth councils, which advise staff on programs, set policies, plan events, and share pertinent information. By including the perspectives of the people who support and use its programs, the Department has effectively moved beyond outreach to a genuine partnership with the larger community.

> "We provided services for 74 cents a kid — it would cost $38,000 per year to lock up a kid."
>
> — Cynthia Peters,
> At-Risk Youth Division Supervisor,
> Phoenix Parks, Recreation and Library Department

CHAPTER ONE

COMMUNITY DEVELOPMENT CORPORATIONS

Community development corporations (CDCs) are organizations that provide housing and economic opportunities to geographically defined groups. Some CDCs also provide other services such as job skills training, educational tutoring, counseling, cultural enrichment programs, and mediating. CDCs are a logical delivery system for cultural community partnerships for two key reasons. First, their constituencies are well defined and are often among the most underserved segments of a community. Second, CDCs have a management structure that can anchor a project logistically. Community development corporations often have financial and business expertise and may have access to resources like neighborhood assistance, tax credits, and community development block grants.

Although CDCs often cooperate with cultural groups, these projects are generally short-lived — such as one-time street fairs. By designing more extended and intensive cultural programs, CDCs can enhance their traditional strategies. *Cultural projects move work from the realm of the economic to the realm of the personal, getting down to the roots of the issues that shape the need for development and redevelopment in the first place.* By employing cultural strategies, CDCs can provide the skills, opportunities, and attitudes necessary to create economic growth.

Portsmouth Community Development Group

Portsmouth, Virginia

A community development corporation that created a Caribbean music program to teach youths life skills.

Portsmouth, Virginia, is a city that is predominantly low-income and plagued by racial problems, but it is also a city dedicated to building a better future. In 1990, the community gathered in a series of town meetings to identify where the city was going and how that might be altered. One of the results was the Portsmouth Community Development Group (PCDG), founded by a group of concerned citizens. Drawing on strong community participation on board, staff, and membership levels, PCDG began by

> "The role of the arts in the social structure follows the need of the changing times:
>
> In a time of social stasis: to activate
>
> In a time of germination: to invent fertile new forms
>
> In a time of revolution: to extend the possibilities of peace and liberty
>
> In time of violence: to make peace
>
> In time of despair: to give hope
>
> In time of silence: to sing out"
>
> — Judith Malina
> *Founder of the Living Theatre*

rehabilitating and selling a score of homes to low- and moderate-income first-time home buyers and by stimulating further renovations by other organizations. Despite initial success in improving the infrastructure of local neighborhoods, however, discussions with com-

CHAPTER ONE

munity leaders revealed that the organization was addressing only a small part of development needs and was not getting at the issues that cause neighborhood decline in the first place. Therefore, PCDG expanded its mission to include arts and culture as a focus, in addition to housing, education, security, youths, and economic programs.

In 1994, to meet PCDG's goal to "help the youth of Portsmouth develop into responsible, self-reliant, creative adults who have a sense of belonging to the community," the organization launched a three-pronged summer arts program. Nine artists from Trinidad came to Portsmouth to introduce local youths to Caribbean pan drums, dance, and interpersonal development. Over the summer, eighty-five youths learned how to create, tune, and play the pan, gained a working knowledge of Caribbean culture and art, and trained in rhythm and movement through dance. A core of students went on to create the Portsmouth Pan Players and have played at more than twenty events during their first year.

While the pan, dance, and general music training provided cultural insights and abilities, the underlying message consistently returned to equipping these young people with life skills. They were taught about discipline, personal responsibility, cooperation, self-reliance, planning, and goal setting. In addition to basic academic tutoring, the program provided the youths with role models and alternatives to delinquent behavior.

This new program has not obscured PCDG's original areas of expertise. The organization has continued to revitalize physical infrastructure, with a new focus on creating incubation space for the arts. PCDG is currently renovating living, working, and exhibition spaces for artists and adapting a vacant storefront into an Urban Arts center with performance and rehearsal space. Expanding the organization's focus to incorporate the arts has not only boosted local exposure to cultural resources, it has strengthened the community as a whole. Many other organizations — such as the police department, other development organizations, parents, and churches — have become involved in the cultural projects and thus have found a new way to rebuild their community.

Cultural community programs come in a broad variety of incarnations; there are many possible ways to design a program and many issues to tackle using cultural resources. Chapter Two outlines a thorough process to determine the best possible approach for specific communities. Chapter Two is highly interactive — there are a number of worksheets to help outline the parameters of a partnership and flesh out the internal work that must be done before an organization or individual can reach out into the community. Creativity is based in action and exchange. The coming chapter offers a preliminary exercise in engaging just this sort of creative problem solving.

BEGINNING THE JOURNEY

CHAPTER TWO

GROUNDWORK:

QUESTIONS TO ASK AND ISSUES TO EXPLORE BEFORE ADOPTING A STRATEGY

The first step in creating a partnership is to understand what sort of partner you or your organization will be. Given the crammed schedules that most of us maintain, there is little time to sit down and think about how day-to-day projects mesh with the specifics of an organizational mission statement or philosophy — let alone about how to integrate a whole new project. This chapter walks through seven essential issues that will help you or your organization define the outlines of a cultural community collaboration:

- Terms
- Critical Issues
- Vision
- Barriers
- Assets
- Opportunities and Strategies
- Future Partners

Each section is teamed with a worksheet that asks the basic

questions necessary to lay the groundwork for partnerships. By recording dreams, what stands in the way, where time is spent, what resources can be donated, and realistic possibilities, it becomes easier to spell out what you are doing, why, and where you are headed.

Initially, you should spend some time defining your own work because successful collaborative projects depend on being able to communicate with your partners. You must know your own boundaries and abilities before you can share them with others. Determining at the outset that as a public entity, your organization has access to excellent equipment but is limited by an earmarked budget, or that as an artist who is unwilling to compromise your creative time, you can only dedicate fifteen hours a week to a joint project, will make it that much easier to negotiate a successful and realistic framework.

These questions apply to both organizations and individuals, so the worksheets can be used either in a group setting — with your staff or board — or individually. They can also be used in initial meetings with potential partners. For those who already have a good sense of the project that they would like to begin and who they want to work with, some of these questions may have clear answers. Nevertheless, going through the exercises will provide convenient summaries that will become instrumental in Chapters Three and Five, the planning and action chapters.

DEFINING YOUR TERMS

Language is one of the first troublesome problems that organizations and individuals face when creating cultural community partnerships, particularly when working with those who operate under different professional and cultural frameworks. *Words as basic as "community," "art," and "culture" can mean very different things to different people.* Although this may seem like an exercise in semantics, looking at your definitions, and being clear about them, will help define the project and its implementation. Understanding from the outset whether you and your partners define these three words differently can also help avoid conflicts stemming from misunderstandings.

COMMUNITY

A community can be defined in any number of ways. It can be a geographical region or a self-identified group. It can be based on ethnicity, spirituality, or close personal ties. For arts managers, community may be a conceptual term. For organizers, it can mean a specific neighborhood, while for public officials it can be seen as constituents and their environment.

Your definition of community reflects how you or your organization approach work and can help identify the targeted group for a project. As a basic step, decide whether to tailor the project to a particular age bracket, ethnicity, religion, economic scale, education level, or geographic area. Choosing specific characteristics can help keep the project limited to a manageable scope and provide a point of reference to ensure that the project content is relevant.

It is important to determine whether your self-identified community and the targeted community are vastly different. If you or your organization have not worked with this community before, having a partner or liaison who is familiar with it will make establishing contact and legitimacy easier (**"An Unequal Balance of Power," Chapter Four, page 56** addresses this issue further). Including someone from the targeted community in the planning processes can also help keep the project grounded in that group, as **"Cultivate Potential Partners," Chapter Three, page 41** shows.

Definitions may also vary for level of involvement. To some, preparing to engage "the community" in a project means gathering leaders from the targeted group. To others it means gathering the opinions and involvement of all the people within that group. Determining the level of community engagement often reveals basic information about how an organization functions and can be used as a springboard for a more in-depth exploration of compatibility with your fellow partners later.

CHAPTER TWO

WORKSHEET ONE
COMMUNITY

1) How do you define the term community?

2) What or who do you define as your community?

3) What community are you targeting?

4) How will you bridge any differences between this community and your own?

5) How do you plan to involve this community?

CHAPTER TWO

ARTS AND CULTURE

While identifying who a project will involve and who it will affect can be relatively straight forward, defining arts and culture — especially for people who are less familiar with creative resources — can be more difficult. Several poles of opinion shape the way that people approach working with arts and culture.

People may have strong feelings about how accessible and integral these resources are to our lives. Art can be thought of as something experienced only on special occasions or as essential to everything we do. For groups that are defining a sense of identity outside the mainstream, art and cultural traditions — such as dance and music — may be seen as very important ways to pass on and celebrate their heritage. However, for others, artistic displays of their culture may not be seen as crucial to their basic identity. Still others may see art as woven into the day-to-day regardless of ethnicity, as a basic expression of human nature. Regardless of your definitions, it is important to be sensitive to the level of integration that seems appropriate to each partner.

Two other poles of opinion are based on whether people see art and culture as active or passive. In the passive view, art and culture are perceived as aesthetic and abstract — objects that are meant to hang in a museum, created by people who lived long ago and far away. This definition can see art as the privilege of the wealthy or the elite, because it demands to be studied before you can understand or enjoy it. In the active view, art can alternatively be seen as something that everyone is capable of engaging with and doing. This philosophy holds that everyone is an artist and that we only need to gather the courage to express our creativity.

While all of these definitions are valid, active, integral definitions are the most helpful when marshaling arts and culture as critical tools for community problem solving. Delving into your own conceptions of art and culture and how you or your organization think that they can be used — together with an awareness of how these definitions may differ for other partners — is a way to determine what type of project you want to undertake together. You may find that you will want to use a new definition or that your organization's definitions are changing over the course of this process.

For example, you may realize that cultural resources are already part of your work or that these assets are close at hand, but that you have overlooked their creative nature because of your definition of art and culture. When community organizations are questioned about whether they use cultural resources, many will respond "no." However, when asked more detailed questions, such as "Do you ever have music at events?" or "Did you have the youths put on a performance?" the answers change. Remembering that culture can be anything from calligraphy to mural painting, rap music to gardening, may open up whole other possibilities for potential projects, resources, and partners.

CHAPTER TWO

WORKSHEET TWO
ARTS AND CULTURE

1) What are your definitions of art and culture?

2) How active or passive do you see art and culture being?

3) How integral are art and culture to everyday activities?

4) How does your targeted group define them?

CHAPTER TWO

IDENTIFYING CRITICAL ISSUES IN YOUR COMMUNITY

Just as people define terms such as community and art differently, people also identify different issues as being most pressing. Knowing what is most important to you or your organization and the full range of issues that you would be willing to work on can help determine common ground with your partner later.

In addition to identifying critical issues, it is important to delve into the forces that shape them. Underlying factors often hold the seeds of strategies that can confront these issues effectively. Three key factors that often shape social issues are

- demographics

- cultural context

- how the issue fits in with other community concerns

For example, if your community is concerned about the rate of teen pregnancy, there are probably a number of elements at play. *Demographically*, girls with poor basic academic skills may be more likely to become teen mothers than girls with strong basic skills. Or pregnancies may occur at a greater rate in particular income brackets.

The *cultural context* of the issue is also important — often issues and their solutions are linked to a set of values. Religion can shape whether teens choose to become sexually active and whether they use birth control, in addition to whether parents will agree to sex education programs. Teen culture, or peer pressure, can also shape decisions. If many young people have their own children by age sixteen, a girl may see pregnancy as normal and not fully understand the consequences to her own life or her baby's if she were to become pregnant.

Finally, it is helpful to know *how this issue relates to other issues in the community*. For example, pregnancy may reflect a sense that teens have nothing to lose by having a child. Looking at the standard of education and opportunities for work and higher learning may reveal both gaps in services and possible resources that could be used as incentives to not become pregnant (examples drawn from Children's Defense Fund, "State of America's Children 1995," **see Appendix B** for more information on this report).

CHAPTER TWO

WORKSHEET THREE
CRITICAL ISSUES

List the key issues in your community in the first column and their demographic, cultural, and community context in the next three columns.

KEY ISSUES	DEMOGRAPHIC CONTEXT	CULTURAL CONTEXT	COMMUNITY CONTEXT
(example: teen pregnancy)	(example: many area residents live below the poverty line)	(example: peer pressure)	(example: lack of mentors promoting higher education)

CHAPTER TWO

CLARIFYING YOUR VISION

Once you have gathered a clear idea of what you or your organization would want to work on and the factors that shape these issues, the next step is to envision how to confront them. This involves identifying both a focus for action and the organizational parameters for this work. The crush of immediate crises that we face at work each day may make it difficult to conceive of inventive, yet manageable, plans for addressing the root causes of social issues. Therefore, it is important to

- think about astute solutions

- take into account how much time this project will consume

- be clear on why you or your organization are undertaking the project

Dreaming big and then allocating appropriate time and energy makes the project more likely to provide innovative solutions and less likely to falter.

CAPTURING YOUR DREAMS

A good way to embrace an innovative strategy is to identify the best case scenario for a critical issue and then determine how to achieve that goal. This form of problem solving hinges on breaking down the limits imposed by what we believe is feasible. *Pondering what has been dismissed as out of reach may trigger new connections and reveal unexpected courses of action.*

The following three-step process can help identify these variables (this information will be important for **"Set Parameters for a Plan," Chapter Three, page 42**). First, record a key problem from the critical issues identified in **Worksheet Three**. Then, imagine a goal — the ideal way this issue could be resolved. Finally, identify a first step that could be taken to reach that goal. For example, a city may suffer from a high rate of failure among new businesses, based in part on the lack of information about opportunities and resources. An ideal solution might be that all new entrepreneurs have free and convenient access to information that would help them avoid commonly made mistakes. One action that can be taken to reach this goal is to create a resource center at the public library.

Forsyth County Library in Winston-Salem, North Carolina, provides an excellent example of how this type of creative problem solving led to a bolder and more innovative vision of the role that a library can play in a community.

CHAPTER TWO

Forsyth County Library

Winston-Salem, North Carolina

A library that undertook a community visioning process to ensure it will be a welcoming resource and community focal point.

Forsyth County Library has a tradition of working in the community. In addition to providing basic literacy programs, the library has an Adult Continuing Education project that helps citizens earn degrees, learn new trades, get financial aid, hunt for jobs, prepare for tests, and gain job and computer skills. The library also houses a collection of materials about North Carolina, works by North Carolinians, rare resources for the study and preservation of local and state history, and a genealogy research section.

However, the library staff felt that the institution was not living up to its potential and wanted to establish a better connection with the community. They applied to be part of the "Public Libraries in Partnership with Communities" program, a joint venture between Partners for Livable Communities, Project for Public Spaces, and the Public Library Association, with funding from the Surdna Foundation.

In order to determine the best-case scenario for meeting local needs, the library sponsored a community visioning process with public and civic leaders. A visioning process uses community participation to clarify connections between economic, social, and environmental factors; prioritize needs; and set agendas to improve them.

The Library's initial, large-scale discussions led to the creation of a smaller steering committee. This committee has two functions. First, it has helped expand the Library's connection with the community and thus become a first concrete step toward the goal of greater participation. Second, it carried out the visioning work necessary to offer new definitions for the Library's role in the community. The committee dreamed of making the Library a center for education, a resource for the business community, a community hub, a connection with technology, and a preserver of local heritage.

To reach these goals, Forsyth County Public Library identified a series of actions. Part of the visioning process made it apparent that the effectiveness of the Library's existing community programs was hampered by the perception that the Library is uninviting and limited in offerings. In order to reenergize its traditional role and anchor its new twenty-first century role, the Library chose to renovate its physical structure and design. The Library will redesign the interior, facade, and surrounding public places to create a more visible, welcoming, and stimulating environment for county residents. In addition, it will be adding new electronic technology and will turn an adjacent building into an expanded history collection and museum to document local heritage. A capital campaign for this work, drawing both public and private support, will begin in 1998. Once completed, the revitalized library facility will better serve an even larger slice of the community.

WORKSHEET FOUR
CLARIFYING YOUR VISION

In the boxes below, indicate a problem that you would like to tackle from the critical issues identified in Worksheet Three. Then, in the Goal box, identify your ideal for how this issue should be resolved. In the First Step box, write one concrete thing that could be done toward reaching that goal.

PROBLEM

GOAL

FIRST STEP

CHAPTER TWO

THE QUESTIONS OF TIME AND ENERGY

One very real limitation on the ability to begin new projects is the burden of existing workloads and responsibilities. There is often a large gap between what we want to do and the time or energy available to put toward these projects. Knowing what causes that gap can help keep a new project grounded in reality (this information will be important for **"The Limits of Compromise," Chapter Four, page 50**).

Factors that affect how much time and energy a project will take include

- whether it is integrated into other projects or if it requires that energy be rechanneled from other programs

- whether a large block of time must be devoted to teaching people about the concepts behind the project and how to implement it

- whether people feel they are being forced to learn about and do the project or if involvement is their own choice

Understanding the scope of time and energy that a project requires lets you begin allocating resources immediately and makes it less likely that you will get overextended. **"Worksheet Five: Time and Energy"** helps outline where your time is already being spent and how the new project can fit into your current workload.

DETERMINING YOUR MOTIVES

In addition to knowing whether you or your organization will have time for a project, you need to be clear about your own motives. Some people or organizations approach joint projects solely as a way to gain new resources and are not interested in entering into the complex process of partnership building. Although effective collaborations allow the partners to pool resources, this gain comes at a cost. The partners must devote energy to negotiating terms and creating an equitable relationship in order to sustain the project for any length of time.

The promise of new resources is also muddied by the evolutionary nature of partnerships. Concrete benefits usually come later on, after the relationship between the parties has been established and they are ready to begin sharing physical resources or to test out a pilot project. Furthermore, joint ventures often develop in forms neither party originally expected as they combine their specific visions. *Partnerships are most rewarding if they are approached as ways to build a support network and to learn new methods of community problem solving, rather than as ways to generate resources.*

WORKSHEET FIVE
TIME AND ENERGY

1) **CURRENT PROJECTS**	**HOW THEY FIT YOUR MISSION STATEMENT**

2) What is the common theme linking them together?

3) Given where your resources are already allocated, where can you insert the new project?

4) How much time will be spent bringing others on board for the project?

5) How will you reallocate your time?

CHAPTER TWO

BARRIERS AND ASSETS

When designing an initiative, time must be spent exploring the specifics of the targeted issue. *It is easy to identify a problem, such as insurance companies refusing to write policies for people in low-income neighborhoods, but it takes a more detailed analysis to identify and address the specifics that shape that problem.* When a community development organization in New York City sought to tackle this very issue in new ways, they discovered both complex roots and an innovative solution.

Neighborhood Housing Services and the Gowanus Arts Exchange

New York, New York

A joint venture between a community development nonprofit and a performing arts organization to introduce theater into pocket parks.

Neighborhood Housing Services (NHS) is a citywide community development organization that increases investment in declining neighborhoods and promotes affordable housing. One problem that NHS confronts in low-income neighborhoods is the reluctance of insurance companies to write policies. Upon studying the issue, NHS found that insurance companies consider vacant lots to be a liability, because they foster crime. Therefore, NHS often works to revitalize these lots as "pocket parks" that may be equipped with a stage or other facilities.

In 1993, NHS joined forces with the Gowanus Arts Exchange to make its pocket park program even more effective, under the auspices of a partnership building program run by Citibank (**see Chapter Four, page 48**, for a description of this program). Gowanus is a Brooklyn-based professional performing arts organization that promotes arts and

CHAPTER TWO

arts education through dance, performance art, music, and theater. It has done extensive work in the community, emphasizing both the importance of performance space for exploration and learning, and the sense of being part of an artistic family.

Together, the two organizations have created "Your Voice Theater," a jointly supervised program for fourteen to eighteen-year-olds in the Bedford-Stuyvesant neighborhood. Participating teens will work with a Gowanus artist-in-residence to explore all aspects of theater arts and to develop a performance. NHS will help select the young people to participate, identify a working space, and create the pocket park where the performance will be. By both giving community residents access to new resources and building their sense of ownership over the park, insurance companies will have several incentives to invest in Bedford-Styuvesant.

For your work, listing the specific concerns that stand in the way can help determine what needs to be done next. There are some issues that are always in the way of doing work, such as time, money, and red tape. Try to move beyond the obvious to the smaller, more subtle concerns that may stand in your way, such as local intolerance toward people who are different, lack of a sense of safety, or key staff who are not supportive of this type of endeavor. **Worksheet Six** pulls out several categories that often hamper initiatives, including those internal to your organization, and social, physical, economic, and political factors. The context for the problem, explored on **page 24, in the "Critical Issues Worksheet,"** may also help identify the root of some of these barriers.

Although there are always things to stand in the way of a project, communities are filled with people and programs dedicated to working on social issues. Most organizations and individuals already have a circle of colleagues that they call upon for information, advice, or assistance. Most communities can also benefit from other resources, such as an active and informed city council or natural resources that pull a strong tourism base. In the Neighborhood Housing Services' case, the Gowanus Art Exchange's strong art and community focus proved to be a valuable resource for anchoring the new pocket park in the community. **Worksheet Seven** will give you a structure for identifying both general and culturally specific resources in your community.

CHAPTER TWO

WORKSHEET SIX
BARRIERS

List factors that stand in the way of the new project that are:

1) INTERNAL TO YOUR ORGANIZATION
(for example: support from board or superiors, time and resource allocation)

2) SOCIAL
(for example: leadership, social service needs, ethnic composition of the targeted community, and how race issues are dealt with)

3) PHYSICAL
(for example: the environment, regulations about building and rebuilding, lack of amenities such as parks, zoos, open spaces, biking trails)

4) ECONOMIC
(for example: tax structure, effectiveness of state and local officials in meeting fiscal challenges, where money is spent)

5) POLITICAL
(for example: lack of support from the local community and leadership)

WORKSHEET SEVEN
ASSETS

List factors that can help the new project that are:

1) INTERNAL TO YOUR ORGANIZATION
(for example: support from board or superiors, time and resource allocation)

2) SOCIAL
(for example: leadership, social service needs, ethnic composition of the targeted community, and how race issues are dealt with)

3) PHYSICAL
(for example: the environment, regulations about building and rebuilding, amenities such as parks, zoos, open spaces, biking trails)

4) ECONOMIC
(for example: tax structure, effectiveness of state and local officials in meeting fiscal challenges, where money is spent)

5) POLITICAL
(for example: support from the local community and leadership)

OPPORTUNITIES AND STRATEGIES

The previous worksheets have identified critical issues, visions for change, barriers, and assets. With the help of these summaries, you can map how these factors fit together and brainstorm on opportunities and strategies. Look at the resources and barriers and see how assets can be applied to wear down the roadblocks. Once the connections become clear, you have the seeds of a strategy.

Knowing the landscape of an issue at this depth may offer some clues for where to look next. If you are a city official looking to revitalize a neighborhood that has a strong historical background, the logical place to start looking is the local historical society, neighborhood organizations (both for citizens and for businesses), and cultural organizations that represent the populations that have lived in this neighborhood. You may also seek out artists who can capture the spirit of the neighborhood for murals, landscape architects to create common space, or cultural institutions that might be relocated or put a satellite facility in the neighborhood to anchor the image, draw tourism, and incubate small service businesses. This example is more than theoretical, as the following case study shows.

The City of Kansas City, Missouri and the Black Economic Union of Greater Kansas City

Kansas City, Missouri

A redevelopment initiative for a historic neighborhood that taps into public, private, and artistic resources.

In 1990, the City of Kansas City, Missouri, passed a $115 million capital improvements bond issue, $20 million of which was earmarked to redevelop the African-American neighborhood of 18th and Vine — once one of the prime sites for jazz in the country and the birthplace of bebop — as a historic district. To capitalize on the area's rich traditions, the City planned to build several museums, restore an old theater, and create new housing units. Rather than launch this project alone, the City designated the Black Economic Union of Greater Kansas City (BEU), a nonprofit community economic development corporation, as codeveloper of residential and commercial properties. The City also held community forums with area residents and local merchants and convened focus groups with schools, artists, and community arts groups that would use the new facilities to ensure that they reflected these communities' needs.

Five years later, BEU has developed nearly ninety units of low- to moderate-income housing. These units will be linked to the arts through outdoor summer jazz concerts and works of art that will be installed on the lots. Incorporating art into housing is only the first step in BEU's plan, however. On property that it owns adjacent to the City property, the organization is also seeking to create an art gallery with student programming and a restaurant serviced by a culinary arts training program.

By identifying and incorporating local people and organizations, the City tapped into several resources. The community meetings served to secure a local mandate and to assure the viability of the redevelopment plans. Designating BEU as codeveloper allowed the City to expand the impact of its efforts. Not only is BEU experienced in this work and this neighborhood, it is already engaging the community through the arts. For over a decade, BEU has hosted the 18th & Vine Heritage Jazz Festival. This festival, which draws a broad range of arts groups, businesses, and community participants in planning and implementation, provides an excellent marketing tool to raise awareness of the redevelopment project and to draw artists and businesses into the neighborhood. BEU benefits as well because it can piggy-back onto the formal structure of a historic district to create year-round cultural and educational outreach programs, thus boosting interest and economic development in the neighborhood.

CHAPTER TWO

WORKSHEET EIGHT
STRATEGIES

Restate the problem and first step from the Vision Worksheet (Worksheet Four). Then review your barriers and assets from Worksheets Six and Seven and develop a strategy.

1) PROBLEM

2) FIRST STEP

3) STRATEGY

FINDING YOUR PARTNERS

Identifying a plan of action makes it easier to take the next step — finding your partners. Cast a wide net in your search; you may be surprised to discover potential partners in unlikely places. *Often there are many people all working on the same issue that are not communicating and therefore duplicating work or missing out on opportunities to share their expertise and resources.* In 1994, for example, Partners for Livable Communities drew together leaders from foundations, cultural institutions, and community-based organizations in San Francisco to discuss how museums and communities can work together to provide support networks for at-risk and overlooked populations. Although some museums were already fully engaged in this effort, many of the community-based organizations were not aware of these endeavors or of the capability of museums to address community needs. Keeping an open mind and exploring connections with a broad range of potential partners may lead to new options for collaborative efforts (this information will help you in **"Cultivate Potential Partners," Chapter Three, page 41**).

In addition to knowing where to look for potential partners, it is important to take into consideration the relationships that already exist between the players in your community. Just as demographics contribute to the problems in our neighborhoods, relationships between individuals and organizations shape the way in which we organize to address these problems. When you or your organization prepare to create a collaboration, it is important to do so with an eye to the power dynamics at play. You may find that some of the considerations that you document here tie directly with the barriers and assets identified in **Worksheets Six and Seven**.

Possible partners include:

- Youth advocacy groups
- Volunteer organizations
- Local convention bureau
- Community theaters
- Neighborhood organizations
- Religious organizations
- Performing arts centers
- Local/state arts agencies
- Musicians
- Corporations
- Libraries
- Historical societies
- Local businesses
- Economic development councils
- Museums
- Parks and recreation departments
- Community centers
- Civil rights organizations
- Teachers and schools
- Division of tourism
- The media
- Community development groups
- Zoos
- Chamber of commerce
- Higher education institutions
- Police departments
- Botanical/community gardens
- Visual artists
- City development agencies

CHAPTER TWO

WORKSHEET NINE
KEY PLAYERS

1) Who are the key players in your community?
(for example: people and organizations in the public sector, volunteer organizations, cultural institutions, community-based organizations, funders, corporate and business leaders, the media, educators, religious groups, and advocacy groups)

2) Who is already doing programs that address the issues that you are concerned about?

3) What do these programs do?

4) What players would you want to work with?

5) How will your project fit into this larger framework?

CHAPTER TWO

NEXT STEPS

Now that you have a list of viable potential partners, you or your organization will be ready to think about how to gather them together. Should you send out a call for these people to come to the next city council meeting, host an informal dinner with other community leaders, or arrange a formal meeting with the executive director of a community foundation?

One way to bring people to the table is to describe the kind of project that you have in mind. In putting forward this plan, however, it is important to avoid being too focused on one particular approach. The work that you or your organization has done over the course of this chapter should supply a set of parameters for what is important to work on and equip you with a list of resources to bring to the table. The next chapter outlines the partnership building process that will prepare you to implement a common plan.

CHAPTER TWO

CHAPTER THREE
COLLABORATION:
STRATEGIC PLANNING AND ACTION STEPS

Cultural community partnerships require considerable planning, gathering of information, and organization before they can launch a program. To be successful, the joint project must meet the needs of the community in a fashion that also suits each of the collaborators, has broad-based support, and can attract funding. This delicate balance can be achieved through a careful planning process, detailed in the following sections:

- Prepare Internally
- Cultivate Potential Partners
- Identify a Flagship Idea
- Set Parameters for a Plan
- Create a Strategic Plan
- Formulate an Organizational Structure
- Solidify Funding

PREPARE INTERNALLY

The beginning of the process is a critical period for all future successes. Lack of organization can result in an over-ambitious beginning, internal divisions, competing, and irreconcilable visions — problems that can derail the process before it has a chance to develop. That is why the **Worksheets in Chapter Two** have you spell out internal definitions, goals, assets, barriers, and plans. When clarifying these parameters within an organization, both staff and board need to be in agreement. This may mean taking time to develop a greater understanding of the value of working in coalition, as well as the value of cross-pollinating the organization's approach with a cultural or noncultural partner. *Many organizations find that a considerable amount of time needs to be spent working internally before they are able to work with other organizations.*

Another crucial thing to identify at this point is who the leadership of this project will be. Most difficult tasks, like collaboration building, occur because of the dedication of one or a few individuals. Identifying a leader also helps to centralize where information is directed and ensures that the project won't lose momentum because no one knows who is responsible for the next step. One important consideration, however, is to avoid becoming inflexible about sharing power and responsibility with future partners by becoming set on having specific people in charge of the whole project.

CULTIVATE POTENTIAL PARTNERS

The next step in building a collaboration is to bring together the potential partners. In order to tap the richest breadth of resources, begin with the project's key issue and identify all of the community leaders who work with this population or on this issue. **"Worksheet Nine: Key Players," Chapter Two, page 38** lays out a strategy for coming up with this list. This is also the first step for a single institution that seeks to become a fulcrum of change — if the organization plans to truly meet the needs of its community, it will need to question that community about its ideas. After figuring out who to work with, establish contact with each of these people or organizations individually. *Beginning with individuals and sharing ideas with them one-on-one lays the groundwork for the relationship building that is necessary to build a strong partnership.* This investment of time may reveal new resources and ideas to bring to an initial meeting, in addition to increasing the likelihood that people will come to an event.

After establishing contact with a range of community leaders, bring them together to discuss how a partnership might evolve. At this point, based on the amount of energy you or your organization intend to expend, you can decide whether to develop a larger or smaller scale partnership. If there is a great deal of interest in the project and a strong base for leadership in other organizations, you may become one of many players in a process. Or you may find that you will have to be the driving force behind any plan, and determine the size of the project accordingly.

IDENTIFY A FLAGSHIP IDEA

Initial meetings work well when six to fifteen people are invited; this range keeps the numbers manageable, while still introducing a diversity of voices. Whatever the total number of people, this meeting will help determine who the core of the partnership will probably be and further the process of building trust and negotiating differences between these parties. One way to set a warm, open tone is to pay attention to the context of the meeting. Be sure that the facility is comfortable and that the meeting time is convenient. Providing food and beverages and setting chairs up in a circle so that people can see each other also help create a more open atmosphere.

CHAPTER THREE

This meeting, in addition to cultivating relationships for future work, becomes a platform for identifying a flagship idea and some possible plans of action. *A flagship idea is a concept around which people can rally to create a more concrete plan.* This idea might be cultivating greater understanding between Black and Asian communities or reestablishing a sense of safety and ownership in a particular neighborhood through a capital improvement project. The **Worksheets in Chapter Two** may be useful tools to help frame this discussion and determine common values.

Once the group has determined the flagship idea, begin brainstorming on ways to address this issue. One good way to gather these ideas, invented by Disney Enterprises, is called "storyboarding." Storyboarding gives people a chance to see, not just hear, how their ideas fit together. This technique is also useful because it allows everyone at the meeting a chance to express their opinions and make clear their priorities.

First, ask all participants to spend five to ten minutes writing down strategies to achieve the flagship idea. Strategies should be written in big print on 8 1/2" x 11" pieces of paper, with only one idea per sheet. Then, have each person tape their solution sheets on the walls under general headings. For example, if the group has agreed to use recreation activities to reach young people who have dropped out of school, the headings might include "sports teams," "arts projects," and "late night programs." Once most of the ideas are up on the walls, group the ideas that are similar and create any necessary new headings. After about forty minutes, this should give a clear picture of several possible approaches. From these possibilities, select a few strategies that can be brought to the larger community or proposed to the participants' organizations.

It will probably take several meetings to solidify the flagship idea, pinpoint strategies, and prepare to include the larger community. Therefore, to keep this process focused, close each meeting by setting the next meeting date and a goal for what will be achieved.

The most successful cultural community projects are grounded in broad-based participation, both from the community that is being targeted and, when creating a collaboration, from partnering organizations. The easiest way to plan a project is to include only a small number of people in the process. This ensures that the plan will have a sharp focus and be less likely to be diffused by trying to accommodate numerous and inconsistent priorities. *But plans designed with a greater breadth of input are more likely to be innovative, effective, and well-supported.* The next step, then, is to seek out perspectives from beyond the key implementers of the plan.

Host a meeting where those interested in or affected by your project can hear about the flagship idea and project scenarios. Open the widest possible aperture to bring in supporters from the outset — invite about three times the number of people sought out for the initial gathering. Be sure to include people and groups that might fund the project, such as senior management from local financial institutions, community development corporations, and businesses. This list should go beyond those who will support it; invite those who may oppose it as well. If these potentially hostile people know that you value their opinion, they may gain a sense of ownership and commitment to the project. This meeting also provides a chance to explain why the partners are using a particular approach, which can be especially useful when trying something nontraditional.

SET PARAMETERS FOR A PLAN

In addition to building support, this meeting will help ensure that the groups' ideas are in line with the needs and desires of the community that will be affected by the project. Neighborhood meetings in Portsmouth, Virginia, revealed that Portsmouth Community Development Group's housing programs did not meet community needs, prompting new cultural programs (**see Chapter One, pages 15 - 16** for a description of this program). Likewise, a larger community meeting may reveal that your plan addresses a symptom rather than a more direct cause of a problem. Or it may show that the plan would work more efficiently with a different age group or over a different duration.

The challenge of these meetings will be to remain open to new ideas, while maintaining the momentum to move forward. One way to keep people moving is to map the discussion visually. This can be done linearly:

Problem ➡ Idea ➡ Strategy

or by showing the way ideas have come full circle:

```
            Strategy I
         ↗           ↘
Strategy II           Problem
         ↖           ↙
            Idea
```

It will probably take more than one meeting to work through all of these issues, especially when a large number of people are involved. In each case, make sure that each meeting is held in a convenient, neutral place at a time when people will be able to come. What these meetings should provide is a set of parameters within which to solidify a plan, much in the way priorities identified in **"Worksheet Four: Clarifying Your Vision," Chapter Two, page 27** shaped the initial planning meeting.

After these larger meetings, the core group should gather to begin planning how to create and put in place a project that meets both the interests of the partners and the needs of the community. This group of partners will need to work on several major topics.

■ **Group composition**

The series of meetings held thus far may not have produced the range of partners that may be necessary for a successful project. Determine whether others should be included in the core planning group and cultivate those relationships if needed. Check back on this issue periodically, as the project matures.

■ **Specifics for the project**

Having gathered partners and bounced ideas off the targeted community, determine the specifics of the project. What population are you targeting? What will you do with them? Where will the work be done?

■ **Funding**

The larger meetings held with the community may have drawn interest from some funding sources. Funding sources may require that the project be shaped in a particular way, so it is wise to begin identifying possibilities immediately, before the project becomes too narrowly defined (**see "Solidify Funding" on page 45** for some ideas).

■ **Division of labor**

Having determined the way in which the project will go forward, decide who will implement which parts of the plan. As **Chapter Four, page 56**, will discuss, resolving this ahead of time can help avert conflicts over money, decisionmaking power, and workload.

CREATE A STRATEGIC PLAN

CHAPTER THREE

■ **Check-in mechanisms**

In order to ensure that process considerations are built into the basic plan, establish check-in mechanisms to periodically allow each of the partners to talk about how they feel the project is going forward and whether their role is still appropriate.

■ **Short-term goals**

With all the work that needs to be done on the process, it is important to have tangible victories early on to keep people excited about the project. Set short-term, easily achievable goals and plan ways to celebrate them.

■ **Long-term goals**

To ensure that the project can be sustained, set longer term goals. Shoot for realistic outcomes that can be reached in one year and in five years.

■ **Build awareness and support for your project**

It is never too early to begin building awareness and support for a project. One of the most effective and inexpensive ways to do this is to cultivate a connection with the media. Although it requires time, this exposure may draw essential funds, community support, and recognition to sustain and energize the project over a period of time.

Clearly establishing how the project will move forward within a defined system is one of the best ways to support it and to lay the groundwork for long-term problem solving. This framework may already exist through an organization or a new one may need to be formed. A structure helps institute the division of labor and check-in mechanisms envisioned in the planning process. It also gives something concrete to point to when seeking additional funding and support. People like to know exactly what they are donating their resources to. *A clear mission statement and plan of action give people a sense of clarity about the project and why it is doing what it is doing.*

Tips for Cultivating a Successful Planning Process

Focus on commonalities of mission, analyze complementary resources, and clearly articulate goals. Having a clear sense of each side's interests and roles makes it easier to develop a plan of action.

Part of visioning is thinking in the positive. Arguments that are couched in what you are for, rather than what you are against, draw less hostile responses.

Be straightforward about tough issues.

Foster friendships and mediate personality conflicts.

Don't assume anyone's position. Don't assume it won't change.

Don't make promises that you can't keep. Be clear about what you can provide.

First impressions are important — these perceptions shape others' realities.

THE ADVISORY BODY

To safeguard the time spent cultivating relationships and a plan of action, it is important to create both advisory and implementing agents for the collaborative project. Advisors can come in many forms. They may be well-known people who add credibility to the program. They may be the people who were engaged in the planning process. Or, they may be an even smaller group that wants to continue being involved in a consulting role. This body will be responsible for offering advice and for advocating for the program. The advisors may also be responsible for evaluating the initial results and

FORMULATE AN ORGANIZATIONAL STRUCTURE

advising on the direction of future efforts. If selected carefully, this team can harness the enthusiasm behind the original plan and direct it to meet the challenges of the future.

THE IMPLEMENTING TEAM

The planning process described above — bringing in a wide array of community leaders and sampling general community opinion — creates a large space to explore new ideas and possible resources. However, once it is time to implement a project, a smaller number of people will be involved. When it comes to the day-to-day running of a program, it is better to centralize management with a few individuals, usually between one and five people. The numbers of people involved will also decrease naturally, based upon how much time and energy the various players have to give.

The implementing team may be made up of different people than the planning body. A new staff person may be hired to carry out the joint project or a more junior staff member may be called in to carry out the program. It is important that these people have a clear understanding of how the community and the partners came to undertake this project and the goals that each collaborator has, in addition to the joint project goal. As "**Developing a Common Plan," Chapter Four, page 48** will explain, it is also important to make sure that the people who will be carrying out the project are given roles appropriate to their strengths and that workloads are distributed reasonably, so that all of their energy can go into making the project a success.

No matter how good an idea is, it is of little use without funding. As the case studies throughout this book have shown, funds can come from a wide variety of sources. One of the benefits of working at the intersection of one or more fields is that it opens new funding categories. *Be sure to look at all the issues that the program is addressing and the communities it is working in for potential sources of support.*

SOLIDIFY FUNDING

Potential Funding Sources

Public sector funds for youth

Schools

Honoraria for presentations

Service clubs

Fraternal orders

Volunteer organizations

Corporations

Local businesses

Foundations

State block grants

In-kind services or donations

Volunteers

Selling items produced by the group, like T-shirts

Federal government redevelopment funds, like community development block grants

Federal agencies like Housing and Urban Development, the Department of Education, or the National Endowment for the Arts

One of the richest and most overlooked sources of information for funding is the library reference desk. Reference desks often have listings of local foundations and other information on project planning resources, such as Lawyers for the Arts or a business bureau that assists in community development. It is also worthwhile to contact local, county, and state governments to find out if there are any assistance programs available. Planning and community development departments sometimes have small budgets designated for grants and technical assistance (**see Appendix B** for more resources).

When approaching a potential funding source, bring a strong statement on the program, including a well-thought-out and detailed budget that documents specific costs. If the project is supported by individuals and organizations, or taps into a pool of volunteers, this information should also be included to demonstrate the viability of the plan. Be sure to show how this program will benefit the potential funder.

When it is time to meet with this funder, send the program's most articulate spokesperson and bring along supporting materials, even if they have been sent to the potential funder beforehand. As described above, potential resources can also be brought in early on to solidify their support and gain their input while the project is still being shaped.

A NOTE ON PROCESS

Although action-oriented, planning does not preclude process considerations. Throughout the planning period, each partner will be engaged in building and strengthening its relationship with the others. Because this process is integral to planning, it should be incorporated into the agenda. Schedule time for the partners to get to know one another at each event and to negotiate different visions, definitions, and working styles. By being straightforward about this aspect of planning, it is less likely that there will be sudden crises of communication or mistrust that can sidetrack the creation or implementation of the project. If the partners develop a strong base for working together, projects can be carried out over the long term. Chapter Four describes the complex dynamics and common pitfalls of partnerships and offers some solutions.

CHAPTER FOUR
TROUBLESHOOTING:
THE NATURE OF PARTNERSHIPS

Each party in a collaboration needs to help foster a genuine dialogue and develop a sense of mutual understanding. In short, they will need to build a relationship. Through joining together to work on a shared vision, each side is opening itself to new expectations, understandings, behaviors, and attitudes. It can be overwhelming to think of expanding to incorporate another point of view, particularly in times when resources are scarce and the climate is one of retrenchment. However, partnerships are well worth the effort because they generate innovative approaches and growth, and strengthen the ability of organizations to survive by providing a wider base of support and access to resources.

This chapter outlines the nature of relationship building between partners. It covers the patterns, phases, and issues that shape the reality of working collaboratively, including:

> Developing a Common Plan
>
> The Limits of Compromise
>
> Translating Across Working Styles
>
> Building Trust
>
> Attention to Process
>
> Distrusting Each Others' Motives
>
> Balance of Power
>
> Division of Roles

DEVELOPING A COMMON PLAN

Leaders and funders from many sectors are learning that by devoting time to the process of relationship building, they are better able to create long-standing, effective partnerships. This has led to whole programs that focus exclusively on the initial planning stages of a project. *When Citibank initiated a partnership planning program, grantees found that a full year is often needed to establish the trust and dedication necessary for effective communication and coordination of logistics.* As Ed Friedman, program director at the Bronx Council at the Arts and a technical assistant to this program, has said, "You can't have an effective collaboration until you know all of the partners' birthdays."

Culture Builds Community: Partnerships for Community Development

New York, New York

A program that offers grants and training to facilitate partnerships between community development corporations and arts programs.

In 1993, Citibank, in cooperation with Partners for Livable Communities, launched a program to develop collaborations between New York City metropolitan area community development corporations (CDCs) and cultural organizations. This initiative, called Culture Builds Community: Partnerships for Community Development, places a heavy emphasis on the building blocks of partnerships rather than on programmatic results. With small planning grants and a series of workshops offered by Brooklyn In Touch and the Bronx Council on the Arts, new partners are given technical assistance in organizational and program development. These workshops provide them with the tools they need to create and implement strategic plans for long-term collaboration by unveiling basic issues such as attitudes, opinions, and past experiences, and providing information and skills on planning, funding, conflict resolution, and teamwork.

Although the focus of the first round was on process, grants were given to organizations that already had the seeds of a project that could be carried out by the end of the year. As the process moved forward, however, it became apparent that the full time period needed to be devoted to relationship building and planning. Even though the grant planners had created the program knowing that a large share of time would need to be spent in planning, the participating organizations discovered that even a year was an ambitious time frame to get a project up and running. Therefore, the second round of training placed a strong emphasis on relationship building and actually discouraged participants from attempting complicated pilot projects.

To capitalize on the groundwork that was laid over the first year, Citibank continued to fund several of the partners in addition to facilitating new joint efforts. One of these enduring partnerships was built among three organizations: the Council on the Arts and Humanities for Staten Island (COAHSI), the Community Agency for Senior Citizens (CASC), and the New York Main Street Alliance (NYMSA). COAHSI is a nonpartisan organization that develops and promotes arts and cultural activities; CASC works with social service agencies and community organizations to assist adults over age sixty to lead viable, independent lives; and NYMSA is an organization dedicated to maintaining the vibrancy of New York's historic commercial corridors by working in partnership with local development corporations.

During Culture Build Community's first year, the three organizations decided to develop a project that would boost economic growth and strengthen the role of cultural institutions in Staten Island's North Shore. The North Shore has a high concentration of economically distressed residents and financially strapped merchants, many of which are losing business to strip malls outside the area. It is also the site of most of Staten Island's cultural resources and a rich collection of late nineteenth- and early twentieth-century buildings. In order to strengthen the link between senior citizens and these local resources, the Staten Island partnership proposed to establish a shuttle bus to travel a cultural loop, encompassing both shopping areas and cultural institutions.

Over a year of planning, three problem areas emerged that are common to most partnerships: communication, time, and logistics. The three organizations discovered that even straightforward messages did not always come through clearly, meaning that a good deal of time had to be spent clarifying these points. In part, this stemmed from the different perspectives that each partner held. NYMSA and COAHSI, because they were not focused on serving the needs of the elderly, needed to learn what this population needed and wanted before the partners were able to tailor a program to them. In addition, all three organizations are umbrella organizations for other institutions. This meant that the small number of staff involved in the partnership had to be very careful to represent the concerns of their constituencies, rather than their personal understandings of the issues.

Because NYMSA and COAHSI consist of single-person staffs, however, they had to weigh how much time they could devote to this project without eclipsing other program areas. Further logistical complications emerged from basic organizational differences between the partners, such as when particular institutions were open, when people could meet, or how to disseminate information. The three partners found that group meetings were often ineffective, particularly when working with the various targeted communities, so they decided to arrange many individual meetings.

At the end of their first year of working together, the Staten Island partners were able to inaugurate a test run of the shuttle bus. Thanks to careful organization and planning, it was a great success. Seniors appreciated the new flexibility that the shuttle offered, and area businesses discovered how they could better meet the needs of older Americans and thus boost their business. Because the project provided a concrete and simple manner for merchants to become involved, it also coaxed new levels of management to work on community development.

The shuttle bus not only benefited the community, it also created a tangible success for the three partners. COAHSI, CASC, and NYMSA will seek funding to continue offering the bus service and are already planning new ways to integrate other projects.

CHAPTER FOUR

THE LIMITS OF COMPROMISE

Like all relationships, partnerships involve compromise. The Staten Island partners had to learn how to balance their individual agendas with the needs of the three represented communities. *Nonetheless, this does not mean that an organization or individual should enter into a project that drains energy from its essential mission and field of work.* Successful collaborations share four key factors

- helping both partners fulfill their missions

- enhancing the quality of each organization's work

- having the support of each group's board

- addressing a mutually identified area of need

The parameters you or your organization have identified for a project, outlined in **"Worksheet Five: Time and Energy," Chapter Two, page 29** should help clarify what would or would not be feasible to undertake.

TAKING TIME TO BUILD A PROJECT

Another important factor in collaboration building is time — time to translate across working styles, time to build trust, and time for the process to evolve. Often, when organizations enter into a joint project, they do so with a strong desire for action, only to be disappointed when things do not run as smoothly or take longer than they originally had planned. As frustrating as this may seem, time must be left for correcting mistakes and for going over issues many times as the partners' positions and perspectives mature and change.

TRANSLATING ACROSS WORKING STYLES

One element that takes time is negotiating across working styles. *This stumbling block may be particularly pronounced in cultural community partnerships, especially if only one party works through a creative process.* The creative process, loosely defined, is a trial-and-error approach. It places a high priority on allocating time for generating new ideas or synthesizing multiple concepts. People using a creative process to solve problems may come up with a main idea, and then improvise several other themes off that idea before coming up with a final product that they are comfortable with acting on. This way of working offers a strong tool for community work because it can generate innovative, unusual solutions.

A process-focused, creative work style can be very difficult to mesh with a more product-oriented approach, however, because it can be time consuming and abstract. Other partners may be more concerned with generating action or producing an outcome that can be quantified with concrete results. Someone using an action-oriented strategy might immediately identify existing resources, lay out a concrete timeline, and assign roles to move a project forward. This way of working is valuable because it is likely to create tangible results. But, it also has its downfalls. Being too product-oriented can mean acting hastily or missing out on opportunities that it would take more patience to find.

The Three Rivers Arts Festival

Pittsburgh, Pennsylvania

An annual arts festival that is creating a public art process that will involve artists, community-based organizations, libraries, and schools.

A clear example of conflict between working styles can be found in the experience of the Three Rivers Arts Festival in Pittsburgh, Pennsylvania. In 1995, Three Rivers hosted a workshop of artists and community activists from around the country to brainstorm on how to redesign the festival to draw greater community involvement. One of the activities at this conference was a role-playing game. The participants were divided into teams, and then asked to solve a problem loosely based on real concerns in Pittsburgh. One group was given the dilemma of what to do with an old mill site on a river, the soil of which was contaminated with arsenic. The participants came up with a plan to turn the site into a community garden/historical landmark. Their solution was to first plant vegetables that leach poisons such as arsenic out of the ground, followed by more attractive or edible plants later. They also proposed that a local neighborhood undertake an oral history project to gather the stories of the people who used to work in the old steel mill. Then posts inscribed with stories and pictures of the workers would be placed at the locations where these people once worked, among the plants.

One of the participants in this group was so excited by the plan that he drove out to the site that night and contemplated how it might be possible to make this a reality. When he informed the group the following day that he would like to move this project forward, however, he was met with considerable resistance. Another participant later declined to present some of his concepts to the rest of the group because he felt that if he did, someone might act rashly on what, in his mind, was just an idea thrown out as part of creative problem solving. The participant who wanted to turn the plan into reality also became frustrated because he did not understand why the people who came up with these plans were suddenly distancing themselves from them.

This experience captures some of the difficulties involved in trying to bridge different styles of planning. In order to be able to work together, the various partners would have to confront their different working styles and come to some sort of agreement on how to work together. *Both need to be able to see the other's way of working as valid and trust the other to take their work seriously.* Then, they can work together to merge the best facets of their working styles to create innovative, viable plans.

One of the best ways to do this is to clearly define the framework and timeline for the project and the process that will be used to achieve it. For example, careful distinctions could be made between time spent brainstorming — when all ideals are valid, but none are written in stone — and action planning — when concrete issues are discussed and agreed upon, and implementation dates are determined.

BUILDING TRUST

Building trust is another time-consuming part of building collaborations. *When the project involves bringing a new player into an established community, people need to know what this new partner is going to do and why.* If there is a history of disinterest or even hostility between the parties, it is especially important to discuss reasons and methods for working together now. Otherwise, new actions will be interpreted through the old framework of doubt, and may be met with suspicion.

Often, trust is built on observing people's actions, in addition to their words. It is also cultivated through sharing experiences, so that people have time to see the individuals behind an organization and a project. Arranging events where the partners can become familiar with each other helps build trust. Another way to help strengthen trust and understanding is to show an interest in the priorities of the other parties and work toward achieving them.

Baltimore City Life Museums

Baltimore, Maryland

An urban history museum, consisting of eight historic landmarks in three inner-city sites, deeply involved in neighborhood revitalization.

The Baltimore City Life Museums have spent more than a decade building strong relationships with the communities in which they are located. Five of the facilities are in Jamestown, an African-American community that sits four blocks from the financial district. Despite their proximity to the prosperous downtown core of Baltimore, the residents of Jamestown face some staggering problems. Ninety percent of children under eighteen live in poverty, 80 percent of households are single-parent homes, and 70 percent of adult females are unemployed.

When the Museums first moved into Jamestown in 1984, they did so without discussing their mission or vision with the residents. Unfortunately, the community interpreted this move as the first wave of a gentrification effort, sparking a summer of vandalism and harassment. Every window of the historic Carroll Mansion was broken, and visitors and staff were harassed when entering or leaving the buildings.

Instead of beefing up security or leaving the neighborhood, the Museums chose to talk with the community about why it had been made a target. Working with the help of a well-respected clergyman, the Museums met with neighborhood leaders and explained the vision that the institution had for its place in the community. Then, the Museums' executive director began meeting with mothers from Jamestown. In discussions that lasted over a year, she talked with these women about her own life and family, and listened to the residents speak about their lives. Eventually, they developed a level of trust that allowed the executive director to ask what the community wanted from the Museums, and she was able to develop a well-supported game plan for doing so.

Today the Museums run a number of community-based programs, including job training for senior citizens and a gallery that gives local residents a chance to document life in inner-city neighborhoods. The Museums are also directly involved with a $1 million redevelopment effort that will reinvigorate a blighted thoroughfare that runs between the Museums and a public housing project. The Museums worked for two years with local residents and small business owners to create the beautification plan and to raise the funds to complete the improvements. Some of this work will be done by local teens, through joint employment and education programs.

By dedicating considerable time and energy to establish trust and understanding with their neighbors, the Museums have become a part of the Jamestown community — to both of their benefits. The community has gained new programs, facilities, and a major redevelopment project. And now, when visitors come to the facilities, they are met by friendly neighborhood faces, rather than with hostility.

ATTENTION TO PROCESS

As a project evolves and changes, attention will need to be directed to the dynamics of the collaboration. *A check-in mechanism should be established to ensure that the arrangement is still working and that people are not feeling overwhelmed by their responsibilities.* Sometimes, this mechanism will seem like a troublemaking activity because it will serve as a valve for tension and conflict. One of the hardest lessons to learn about coalition building is that conflict is not necessarily bad. Voicing differences of opinion — even strong differences — can allow partners to discover underlying concerns and to work through the point of contention, rather than having resentment erode the relationship between them. Knowing what is at the heart of tension makes it easier to resolve the problem in a way that is acceptable to all parties (**see "Launching an Initial Program," Chapter Five, page 61** for more information on conflict).

> **The following exercise illustrates the effort that building a collaboration takes:**
>
> Take both hands and clasp them together so that your fingers entwine. Take note of whether your right or left thumb is on top. Now re-clasp your hands so that the other thumb is on top. Notice how this feels. You may find it awkward, requiring conscious effort and more time than what you would naturally do.
>
> The early stages of a collaboration, and the transition points as you negotiate conflicts and changing expectations, feel a lot like having the less-comfortable thumb on top. It is important to remember that this does not mean that the partnership is failing. It means that you are stretching to do things in new ways.
>
> *(Reprinted with permission from Brooklyn In Touch Information Center, Inc.)*

Another factor that contributes to conflict is fear. Changing the way an organization conceives of an issue and introducing new organizational processes can be fundamentally threatening. Most people resist change when it comes to the issues and patterns that they hold most dear. Some of these fears may be legitimate checks on what is being asked of them. As **"The Limits of Compromise" on page 50 and "Worksheet Five: Time and Energy," Chapter Two, page 29** illustrated, it is important to define and stick by one's own limits. Other times, it may take a period of gaining trust and developing a better understanding of why something is happening before a resistant person is ready to move on in the process of creating a project. *The best way to handle resistance is to determine how that person's concerns can be addressed and then decide whether this is a effort that the other players would be willing to make.*

Finally, as a partnership evolves, it may mature in ways that the partners did not expect and focus on different issues than they initially hoped to address. The partners may discover that there is another issue that they are better suited to work on. Or, they may have more resources at their disposal than they originally thought. They may find, as the Staten Island partnership did, that the investment made in the relationship between organizations leads to a spirit of collaboration that extends beyond a particular project and results in new constellations of program coordination.

Cultural Collaborative Jamaica

Jamaica, New York

A partnership of cultural groups, businesses, a university, and a development corporation that uses cultural resources to address community issues.

In 1993, Cultural Collaborative Jamaica received funds from Citibank's Culture Builds Community partnership program to implement the Jamaica Jubilee Spring 1994 Festival. The Festival was intended to highlight the rich culture and heritage of the Jamaica community and especially to involve local youths. The Jubilee was also a testing ground for the Collaborative's new partnership.

Cultural Collaborative Jamaica originated with four organizations — Greater Jamaica Development Corporation, Jamaica Art Center, York College, and the historic King Manor — that recognized their common interest in quality-of-life issues. With the help of a major grant from the Arts Forward Fund, they had been able to carefully plan and create a community network to apply cultural resources to community concerns. At the time that the Collaborative began the Citibank project, it consisted of eleven organizations, including visual and performing arts organizations, a farmers market, a library, and historical organizations.

After a year of considerable work, the Jubilee was a smashing success. The grant came to a close, and the organizations hired Partners for Livable Communities to facilitate a workshop. This workshop allowed the collaborators to examine their work as a team, to pinpoint what worked well, and to determine how the Collaborative could be improved.

Discussion revealed that some members felt the joint project had taken more time than they anticipated, and that they might not have the financial or staff resources necessary to carry out a festival the following year. A strong feeling also emerged that the Collaborative should facilitate the member's programming and not duplicate the individual organizations' events. Rather than dismiss partnerships as being too much of a drain, the Collaborative members used their new, more realistic understanding of coalition work to come up with a better plan.

First, they decided to create a chart so the partners could document their desired form and level of participation. Three columns allow the members to choose whether they will assist in governance, coordination and implementation, or staff and monetary support. Another column records whether they will serve as presenters or if they will provide a venue for programs. While this agreement is left flexible, so that organizations can change their level of involvement as needed, it serves as the framework for consensus and collective commitment to roles and responsibilities.

The chart serves several functions. It forces the members to think through what and how much they are willing to give to the Collaborative. It also is given to each of the partners, so they know who to call on if they need a service the others can provide. Finally, it serves as a standard to measure involvement against. By periodically reviewing what everyone agreed to do, compared with the actions actually taken, the partners can assess how well they are supporting and using the program.

Second, with funding secured from the New York Community Trust, Consolidated Edison Company, and Chase Manhattan Bank, the Collaborative members decided to hire a full-time staff person. In order to assist each member organization and facilitate common projects, this staff person coordinates small-scale programs, strengthens the members' partnership building skills, and gives each organization individual technical support.

The workshop, in addition to clarifying areas for improvement, also underscored the group's successes. The members found that sharing resources and information was especially helpful, so they decided to strengthen cross-fertilization efforts. For example, the Collaborative created "On the Avenue" — a program that uses funds donated by the Greater Jamaica Development Corporation to give matching grants to Collaborative members for performance projects. These grants have several guidelines: they must use a cultural partner; they must take place in downtown Jamaica; they must provide a draw for daytime employees in that area; and they cannot be held in the recipient's building. Projects that are joint ventures between Collaborative members are given extra consideration. By putting parameters on the funds, the Collaborative is able to ensure that the programs follow the group's goals: to promote culture and local resources; to strengthen the member organizations; and to enhance their cooperative work.

WHY SOME PARTNERSHIPS FAIL

Coalition building takes a considerable amount of skill in consensus building, communicating, and educating. Many organizations that have attempted joint efforts discover that their collaborations collapse because neither party was aware of the amount of work it would take or was prepared to endure rough periods as each side defined and clarified their roles. Others fail because the partners cannot secure funding, do not have the time to invest in them, the authority to make the commitment, or relevant skills and resources to offer. Finally, partnerships may unravel because the collaborators are too different to be able to work well together. In cases like these — where the partners were not fully prepared to work together — failure is almost always inevitable. However, some of the issues over which viable partnerships fail — such as distrusting motives, the balance of power, and the division of roles — can be addressed and resolved.

DISTRUSTING EACH OTHERS' MOTIVES

One of the first problems that partners may encounter is distrust over motives. Given the assault that cultural institutions are facing on the national front and the budgetary restraints affecting them on the local level, community groups may assume that a cultural institution only wants to do a collaborative project as a ploy to maintain funding. For their part, cultural institutions may see community groups as trying to take advantage of their resources and subverting their mission to other causes. It will take time for the partners to develop a level of trust about motives. *Being able to talk openly and honestly about why each partner is undertaking this project is one of the best ways to cope with feelings of distrust.*

AN UNEQUAL BALANCE OF POWER

One important issue for sustaining a program is the balance of power between partners. Ideally, we would want to share power fifty-fifty, but this rarely works for day-to-day tasks. As the project evolves, different partners will have a larger role to play. One organization may be instrumental in negotiating the logistics for a program, while another may be the main coordinator of its implementation. When planning a collaboration, take into account each party's area of expertise and sphere of influence. Then decide how to balance out existing inequalities so that all partners feel adequately represented. Having clearly defined roles and rules will help make this balancing easier.

Partnerships break down when one partner feels it doesn't have enough say over how the project is evolving. Two key factors that feed into this balance are money and decision making power. *Although this may seem obvious, it is important to remember that if one party holds the majority of the resources or makes most of the decisions, it has greater power to shape how the project evolves.*

Inequality in resources and decision making is more likely when there is a disparity between the partners' scopes of influence. If only one organization has traditionally worked with large budgets or run sophisticated fund drives, it would be natural to have that organization be in charge of finances. When this choice is made, the partners need to be aware that the already-existing difference has been made larger. They may need to counterbalance this division of labor by ensuring

Essential Components to a Collaboration

Trust

Respect

Flexibility

Accountability

Cooperation

Patience

Hard work

Financing

CHAPTER FOUR

that the less experienced partner will have a role in all major financial decisions. The same double-weighting can happen with decision making in general. Those who are used to holding a position of authority, such as a city official or the director of a museum, may assume a managerial role and further remove those who have had little power, such as artists or community organizers, from decision making.

Nevertheless, the partners do need to recognize each player's realm of expertise and how these various perspectives can be integrated into the project. Someone not used to the expectations of the business world may have to defer to a more experienced partner about the way documents should look or how material is presented. If one partner is more familiar with the targeted community, the other collaborators may rely on that party for information on how to introduce concepts or what hidden factors are shaping situations (**"Defining Your Terms," Chapter Two, pages 19 - 22** offers guidance on bridging gaps between communities). The Downtown Arts Project, working in Harlem, offers one model for a healthy balance between recognizing skills and maintaining equality.

Def Dance Jam Workshop

New York, New York

A dance and theater program for deaf and hearing teenage girls that draws on school, church, and artistic resources.

In the summer of 1994, Downtown Art Co., a small professional arts company in lower Manhattan, approached Aziza, a Harlem-based professional dancer and teacher fluent in American Sign Language, to develop a joint project. Aziza conceived of Def Dance Jam Workshop (DDJW), a dance and theater program for African American teenage girls — half of whom are deaf. DDJW covers a broad range of issues. Members create and perform new works that incorporate sign language, drumming, original writing, African, hip-hop, and modern dance. They also participate in workshops on issues such as self-defense and HIV, go on field trips, and take on community service tasks.

With the help of several other partners — a local dance studio, a junior high school for the deaf, a church, and members of the arts community — Downtown Art secured funding, rehearsal and performance space, costumes, video services, and workshop presenters. After the program's premiere performance at the Judson Memorial Church in Greenwich Village, Canaan Baptist Church and the New York City Mayor's Office for People with Disabilities added their support to enable the project to continue.

Creating a program that spans both the hearing and deaf communities mandated some structural divisions of labor and responsibility, especially given that the Downtown Art staff did not know sign language. Downtown Art depended on Aziza to translate and be the main connection to deaf company members, collaborators, and audience members. On the other hand, Aziza had to rely on Downtown Art's experience in developing projects that link arts and community to get the program off the ground. Downtown Art translated between staff and funders, the business community, and the churches.

The DDJW partners created a clear and open decision making structure to bridge their different areas of expertise and to ensure that all actions were made with joint approval. The budget was designed jointly, using Downtown Art's fiscal experience to create detailed line-items. Although day-to-day control over money was given to Aziza, any deviations from these line items were cleared with Downtown Art. This gave Aziza new experience with working through a budget, while making sure that she could explain why she was making specific decisions. Thus, both partners remained involved with monetary issues.

Conversely, Downtown Art was given primary responsibility for generating the resources to run the project. When the organization identified new parties who could provide cash or in-kind services, the two partners jointly designed the terms for the role that these new entities would play.

By focusing on the areas in which each held the most expertise, while still sharing these responsibilities, Aziza and Downtown Art were able to create an effective, balanced project. Aziza was able to learn new fiscal skills and Downtown Art gained a new understanding of and connection with the deaf community. Both were able to actualize their vision of working with youths through the arts and have created a meaningful program that will endure.

AN INAPPROPRIATE DIVISION OF ROLES

Another aspect that makes the balance of power and responsibility difficult is what gets asked of each partner as they extend into new roles (clear and appropriate roles are especially crucial for **"The Implementing Team," Chapter Three, page 45**). When an artist is brought into community work, or someone used to addressing social issues engages in an artistic process, their work skills may not readily apply to the new situation. They may be required to grapple with unfamiliar problems or encounter inexplicable behaviors. Because the success of cultural community projects relies so much on process, what happens day-to-day is a major factor in whether the project achieves its goals.

If the person who carries out the daily work cannot stay on top of both the creative project and the impact that it is having, participants often drop out of the program or large blocks of time are taken from working on the cultural aspect of the project. One of the balancing acts in cultural community projects is both addressing social issues and creating a quality artistic or cultural experience. Unfortunately, it is rare that people have both strong cultural and group process skills. Therefore, the project planners need to decide whether there should be several people present to work with the targeted population.

Multiple leaders may be necessary when the person who will be carrying out the project comes from a significantly different neighborhood, socioeconomic class, or ethnic group than the targeted population. When people working in the field are unfamiliar with the values and structural factors that shape the community with which they work, they may need to have someone present who can serve as both a translator with that population and a confidante to process this new experience. *By building in someone who knows and can explain both sides' patterns of language and behavior, more energy can be focused on the project itself, rather than trying to figure out why concepts are not getting across or why participants are not showing up.*

When working with troubled youths, it is important to have someone familiar with child development and social work present in the program. Artistic endeavors, because they call on the emotions, can evoke strong feelings and actions. This person can help work through problems — such as a disruptive participant — and determine outside factors that may be shaping a problem, such as potential child abuse.

Think through what each partner will be asked to do, ensure that there is adequate support planned, and have periodic check-ins to make sure that this plan is still appropriate. Sangre Latina, a project working with Latino youth, illustrates how assigning roles carefully can help build a successful project.

Sangre Latina

Richmond, California

A theater program, run by a psychologist and an actress, to further at-risk Latino youths' commitment to higher education.

In 1993, the California State Department of Health hired actress Luz de la Riva to create a play about the dangers of tobacco with high school students in Richmond, California. Richmond, an industrial city in the Bay Area, is a predominantly African-American community, with a pocket of Latinos. A group of Latino students, mostly gang members, began coming to rehearsals and became so invested in the program that when it was over, and they were told it wouldn't continue, they vandalized de la Riva's car. Rather than respond in anger, de la Riva realized how important the program was to the lives of these students. With the help of Luz Estela Rebelo, a psychologist, and funds from the Health Department and a Latino family social work organization, they created Sangre Latina, which means "latin blood." Sangre Latina trains young people in theater arts, including writing, technically producing, and performing plays for other students. By providing skills and a context for success, the Sangre Latina keeps teens off the street, improves their school work, and enables them to aspire to higher education.

The two women who run Sangre Latina are working with few resources. They both hold other jobs and have pieced together further operating funds from donations, a small foundation grant, and their own bank accounts. They also are faced with helping youths cope with devastating problems. They have rescued teens from the street at 2:00 AM and kept others from running away. When a 15-year-old girl was found raped and murdered in an elementary school in a gang-related incident, the two youth workers counseled and held discussions between gang leaders to prevent further violence. This program has become successful because both partners understand that working with the students could not be done on a purely artistic level. They built into their vision of the organization the need to address the psychological and physical crises that these youths face.

Partnership building between cultural and community-oriented parties is a balance between process and action, drawing on the strengths of several approaches. This chapter outlined many of the relationship building and balancing issues that underlie the success or failure of a project. Chapter Five explains how to launch an initial project, measure its success, and ensure its longevity.

FROM PROCESS TO ACTION

CHAPTER FIVE
ACTION:
CARRYING OUT YOUR PLAN

So far, we have seen that exhaustive planning can help get a cultural community collaboration off to a successful start. If each partner has put a great deal of time into building relationships with each other and as a result, bettered their own work, the project is likely to last past its pilot stage. A number of other mechanisms can also be put into place to move from ideas to action, and then sustain a program in the long term. Starting with a relatively simple project, making an honest and thorough assessment of this program, establishing a course for leadership, and strengthening a base of support are all basic steps in creating a sustainable project. This chapter discusses how to carry out these steps, through:

- Launching an Initial Program
- Recording Participation
- Questionnaires
- Recording the Process
- Combating Social Problems
- Using Assessment Methods from Other Fields
- Formal Evaluations
- An Institutionalized Approach to Leadership
- Building Support

LAUNCHING AN INITIAL PROGRAM

Launching an initial program is an exciting time because the fruits of hard work are finally within reach. Yet this time also holds its own difficulties, and careful handling is needed to keep the fruit from being damaged as it is harvested. Successful collaborations are more likely when the partners follow five guidelines:

■ Maintain a process mechanism

Moving forward will put the partnership to another test because the collaborators will have to assume new roles. Once again, allocate time and keep communication lines open so that the partners keep in touch with each other and can evaluate how the project is moving forward. It is also helpful to share information in general; the partners may soon find that they can assist one another in many small, simple ways.

■ Start small

One of the best ways to make this transition is to start with a small project that has easily attainable goals. This may be a joint, one-time activity, a scaled version of the plan, or the first step in a large, complex process. Think of the first project as an investment in the future; being successful at something small will greatly improve the chances of one day succeeding in some grand fashion. Beginning modestly also helps formalize the concept that not all problems can be solved immediately. Sticking to realistic goals makes people less likely to get discouraged and walk away from the project.

■ Leave room for mid-course corrections

Once the plan rolls into action, it is almost inevitable that the partners will have to alter their course and timetable to take into account unforeseen elements. This is also why having an implementing team is helpful — it can channel this information to the various partners and give an avenue for response. Many partnerships need a mid-course correction, even to the degree of redefining their goals. This is all part of a healthy, dynamic process.

■ Permit conflict and work toward its resolution

Another part of a healthy process, as outlined in **"Attention to Process," Chapter Four, page 53**, is conflict. Through conflict, the partners are able to clarify their own positions and truly integrate different perspectives and approaches. Although frightening, it can lead to positive change. There are many books that describe the evolution of organizational conflict and how best to resolve it (**see Appendix B** for a list of resources).

■ Celebrate successes

Once a project achieves its initial goals, it is very important to identify successes and celebrate them. Working on social issues can be grueling, making it all the more meaningful to recognize the efforts that people make to better the lives of those around them. Crediting both the individuals that shoulder projects and the communities that grow through these efforts offers a chance to rest, feel good, and reenergize so that you can move on to bigger and broader projects.

Tips for Implementation

- Start small
- Divide the workload
- Have easily attainable goals
- Celebrate successes
- Ensure mutual benefits

Basic Conflict Resolution Steps

- Distinguish points of potential resistance
- Define the nature of this resistance
- Identify sources that can be realistically influenced
- Determine strategies for doing this

(reprinted with permission from Brooklyn In Touch Information Center, Inc.)

61   CHAPTER FIVE

VARIOUS MODELS OF ASSESSMENT AND DOCUMENTATION

elebrating is one way to move the project forward from an initial joint effort to a more complex or long-term program. Another tool is an assessment process. *Assessments can help ascertain strengths and weaknesses, provide guidance for improvement, evaluate impact and accountability, and increase understanding of the process involved in building a collaborative cultural community program.* This provides a basis for future planning and ensures that the partners are doing the sort of work that everyone agrees is important. As part of this assessment, it is also helpful to document the impact of the program. Putting these results in more quantitative terms can help bring potential funders forward. The following sections identify some of the many possible ways to assess and document a program.

RECORDING PARTICIPATION

One basic assessment tactic is to record the content of the program and the number of people that are affected by it. Although simple, this is the kind of information that most people want to know about a program. Being able to say that 200 students studied dance, music, and theater in an after-school drug and alcohol prevention program shows that this program was both well attended and employed artistic measures to tackle a critical social issue. These numbers can also be used to track whether certain programs grow more or less popular over time, to determine if changes need to be made.

Artists Collective

Hartford, Connecticut

A performing arts center, strengthening knowledge of African-American heritage and building life skills through performances and classes.

The Artists Collective — a multi-arts cultural organization located in a former Hartford school — was spearheaded in 1970 by Jackie McLean, an internationally acclaimed alto saxophonist, composer, and educator. McLean, who spent eighteen years fighting an addiction to drugs, conceived of the program as a means to fight substance abuse. As the Collective has evolved over the past quarter century, however, it has created programs that address the full spectrum of human potential. Often referred to as an oasis in the poverty-stricken North End, the Collective encourages young people to go to college, provides alternatives to drugs, creates a family-style support network, grounds the community in its African/Caribbean heritage, and trains young people in critical thinking, self awareness, and self-esteem.

In addition to classes in dance, drumming, music, drama, visual arts, and martial arts, the Artists Collective provides job training with the City of Hartford. The World Of Work summer program includes presentations by adult role models from a variety of local agencies and businesses on employment, health education, and cultural awareness. Both World of Work and a similar year-round program also train young people in basic pre-employment skills. These classes are intended to give teens a sense that employment is more than a job; it also requires a work ethic and a commitment to well-being.

The Collective keeps statistical data on all people who take part in programs, including geographic information, age, ethnic origin, and gender. Records are also kept on how many people attend the performances put on by participants and by a host of world-renowned performers. All departments and workshops chronicle the number of people who participate, and monthly reports are created on their activities. Since the organization has existed for more than two decades, this sort of information is especially impressive. Many programs can be pointed to as a point of contact with hundreds of young people, and every performance hundreds more over the past twenty-five years.

These statistical data have been particularly helpful in raising support for a new facility. The Collective is in the midst of a $7.9 million building project to create a new, more sophisticated space in a nearby neighborhood. The Collective's extensive archives have greatly strengthened the argument that a larger and better equipped building is needed to serve the numbers that utilize the organization's outstanding programs.

QUESTIONNAIRES

Another way to receive feedback on the success of the program is to distribute questionnaires to participants or the targeted community. Basic questions can be drawn up using the project goals. For example, in the case of the Staten Island project that provides transportation for elderly people to reach cultural institutions and to make better use of local shopping opportunities, separate questionnaires might be drawn up for the people who ride the bus, local merchants, and the staff of cultural institutions (**see Chapter Four, pages 48 - 49** for a description of this program).

The form for seniors could ask whether the shuttle services the destinations they want to reach, whether having the shuttle made them more likely to shop nearby rather than in suburban strip malls, and what benefits they received from visiting cultural facilities.

The questionnaire for shop owners could ask if their business had increased because of the shuttle route, what types of products seniors have purchased and how accessible they were, and whether the stores could make other changes to better accommodate the needs of seniors, based on their recent experiences working with that population.

The form for cultural institutions could ask what cultural events riders attended, whether programming could be changed to better meet their interests, and if the program had boosted the profile of the arts in the community.

By determining whether the program met the partners' goals and raising questions about how the program could be further improved, questionnaires can both give valuable feedback and help move the project to new levels of effectiveness.

Assessments may use an internal reference point, such as exhaustively recording the process that participants go through, to document and judge the effectiveness of a program. Project staff may write down everything that happened over a period of time, analyze the day's proceedings using a structured set of questions with colleagues, or even ask the participants to record their own observations. This approach is time consuming, but it provides the most detailed report of what works, how participants are responding, and how people evolve over the course of the program. It can be especially useful during the pilot phase of a project — where every shred of evidence will help create a more permanent program — or for work that is largely focused on process rather than outcome.

RECORDING THE PROCESS

Living Stage Theatre Company

Washington, D.C.

An improvisational theater company that works with people who are at risk, emotionally disturbed, and physically disabled.

For almost thirty years, Living Stage Theatre Company has used improvisational performances based on strong social themes to give teen mothers, emotionally and physically disabled children, prison inmates, and people from high-risk, low-income neighborhoods a vehicle to understand and control their lives. The Company works to create a safe environment in which participants can cultivate creative problem solving and conflict resolution skills, and encourages resistance to drug use and other destructive behaviors. Many of these programs are strengthened by and grounded in partnerships with local social service and education agencies.

Because improvisational theater is such a creative and varied activity — no two productions are ever the same — it is very difficult to apply a standardized evaluation to the program. This is made more complicated by the interdisciplinary approach that Living Stage takes. Grounded in human development principles, the process that each individual participant goes through becomes the most important outcome of each activity. Therefore, the program uses a contextual assessment process.

After each workshop, the members of the Company evaluate their work through guidelines based on the organization's highly detailed philosophy of creativity as the root of learning, expression, and health. The staff also track whether they were able to maintain a positive environment — built on a sense of safety, respect, and freedom to express oneself — necessary for participants to truly engage in the work.

Further assessment is done for individual participants. Because most of Living Stage's work is done with troubled children, elements such as eye contact, ability to relate to others, and health are often primary indicators. The Company records what each participant did over the course of the day and, using previous contact as a reference point, assesses how the creative process is affecting that person and how to proceed.

These findings are also recorded in reports, some of which are intended for those outside the organization, such as a school that is referring students to the program. External reports begin by explaining the essential factors in human development and how the creative process affects growth, particularly in children. Then they give a summary of the work done by the group and profiles of each participant, including a description of the challenges each faced and how this led to growth. Anecdotes are often used to illustrate this transformation.

Internal reports are used to document the techniques that work, recommend new courses of action, record what the staff has learned from the children, and continue the process of developing and training Living Stage Company members. Just as the creative process is always evolving and providing new insights, Living Stage believes that its work continues to build and grow from understanding the content of daily experiences.

COMPONENTS TO ASSESS

Scale and efficiency

Comprehensiveness and integration

Orientation to recipients

Cost effectiveness

Outreach success

Adaptability and flexibility

COMBATING SOCIAL PROBLEMS

Measuring how staff and participants feel about a program is an internal assessment. It works entirely within the framework that was designed for a specific plan of action. Another way to assess a program is to measure it against external factors. One external assessment method is to document how a program affects social issues that are generally accepted as critical, whether in economics or in human development. Describing a program in these terms is a form of translation — it allows those who may not see the value of cultural community work to understand its benefits for their own concerns. These descriptions can also assist program planners, describing how arts affect social concerns can help maintain a focus on the community side of a cultural community project.

Artspace Projects, Inc.

Minneapolis, Minnesota

A nonprofit real estate developer, working to create physical space for the production of art within a community setting.

Artspace Projects, Inc. is a nonprofit real estate developer that transforms old buildings into safe, affordable space for low- and moderate-income artists. Although based in Minneapolis, where it created its first three live-work-exhibit-rehearsal-performance spaces, the organization now consults nationwide in both urban and rural communities. In each project, Artspace seeks to help artists become more self-sufficient and further integrated with the larger community through development and service efforts.

Artspace springboards off the issue of neighborhood revitalization to make its voice heard outside the arts community. It argues that in order to rebuild neighborhoods, communities need to rekindle a sense of common values, identity, spirit, and vision — in short, to create human structures to support the physical structures that we build around them. Art, as a basic human experience, serves to erect these very structures by creating a tangible representation of identity and meaning, and a means of communication. The joint arts/living spaces that the organization develops provide both the vehicle for community building and the location for doing this work.

Artspace's argument has not fallen on deaf ears. The organization has provided consulting services in fifty communities on real estate development, community building, diversity in the arts, and neighborhood development and the arts. With funding from the Pew Charitable Trusts, Artspace will host a series of conferences on community development and the arts. It has also launched a program focused on long-term rural development with a grant from the Bush Foundation.

Highlighting the role of neighborhood revitalization does not simply help attract further projects — it helps keep existing facilities focused on their original goals. It is ultimately this first hand knowledge that fuels Artspace's continuing efforts to put arts to work on community problem solving.

CHAPTER FIVE

USING METHODS FROM OTHER FIELDS

Another form of external assessment is to borrow evaluation methods used in specific professional disciplines. By adapting a recognized form of analysis — particularly one that can assign numbers or apply terms that are well known — a project may gain credibility within that given professional field. For example, an arts-based drug and alcohol abuse intervention program can use a traditional intervention evaluation to show how arts are an effective tool in this field. This form of evaluation also ensures that the program remains true to its goals of abuse prevention.

Project Self Discovery

Denver, Colorado

An arts-focused program, strongly grounded in psychological theory, that helps drug-addicted youths remain off drugs.

Drugs are a two-edged peril for young people. Not only do they damage the user's body and our society, they create unrealistic expectations for how intense life should feel. Seeking to keep high-risk teens clean, Project Self Discovery (PSD) has married psychological theory and creative expression. This innovative program gives addicted youths a means to attain a "high" without alcohol and drugs, by engaging them in drama, music, dance, martial arts, and visual arts. This exposure to the arts is teamed with intensive counseling and drug education.

Project Self Discovery is a three-tier, 36-week early intervention program, funded by the Center for Substance Abuse Prevention and housed in the Cleo Parker Robinson dance studios. When students enroll in the program, they receive state-of-the-art information on biological, psychological, and social aspects of substance abuse and study an artistic or physical skill. During the "Graduate Program" phase, the youths engage in leadership training and create a performance reflecting teen triumph within the context of widespread violence, substance abuse, and social uncertainty. The final segment, "Mentorship," allows graduates to serve for twelve weeks as paid peer instructors to new participants. As a result, these students display fewer problems with school, family, mental health, drug use, deviant behavior, and negative peer influence.

PSD adapted the "multifactoral quantitative assessment" process, used for adolescent alcohol and drug abuse programs, to measure its effectiveness in changing behavior. When teens enter the program, the staff identifies risk factors (such as rebelliousness, poor parental involvement, and living in a community where drug use is prevalent) and protective factors (such as resources for jobs and recreation, leadership opportunities, and a supportive social network) that affect the teens. These factors are monitored over the course of the program and measured at the end to determine any change in the participants. The staff measure outcomes through their own observations, reports from the teens, observations from people who are important to the youths, and analysis of school and criminal records. All statements are recorded through standardized surveys to create a measure of consistency. The results are then compared to a group of students who did not participate in Project Self Discovery.

PSD also tracks teens who have gone through the program over time, to gain further statistics on its effectiveness. At six and twelve months, former participants answer a battery of questions through a structured interview and questionnaire. The staff who administer these follow-up sessions then rate how prevalent the risk factors have become again and complete a checklist that measures some resiliency factors. Records are also kept of each participant's involvement with PSD, both during and after the formal program.

Project Self Discovery's use of established methods has had several benefits. The program has gained credibility within the drug and alcohol intervention field, and the impact of PSD's arts strategy has been documented in a professional journal. Equally important, the program has a clear record of how it has affected the lives of the young people that it has come in contact with. These data can be folded back into PSD's planning so that it remains on the cutting edge of drug intervention strategies.

FORMAL EVALUATIONS

Given the current push by foundations and other charitable donors to require quantitative evaluation, it is particularly important for programs using cultural resources to develop an assessment tool that puts an essentially qualitative experience into more quantitative terms. Foundations may mandate that grantees hire an outside, impartial consultant to evaluate the program. In this case, success is determined through observation, studying relevant documents, and gathering information from participants and staff through interviews and questionnaires. Professional evaluations are often very expensive, so this cost should be included in the initial budget.

Whichever method you choose, assessment tools should encourage experimentation, leave room for failure, check against the project goals, steer the initiative toward what works, and measure real outcomes.

How does a project maintain long-term vision, interest, and action? In large part, by continuing forward using the tools that have been outlined in the last three chapters. As the project evolves, however, there are some other factors that should be taken into consideration.

AN INSTITUTIONALIZED APPROACH TO LEADERSHIP

Inevitably, leadership changes over time. Unfortunately, when the person who was the moving force behind a project leaves, the collaboration often begins to unravel. But this is not inevitable. A project with a long-term vision can nurture new, up-and-coming leaders to help ensure continuity.

The first step to continuous cultivation of leadership is to depersonalize it. As long as a project is seen as the creation and vision of one individual alone, it is automatically limited to the parameters of that one person. It is also extremely difficult to maintain a balanced partnership under an oligarchy of one. *If the concept of leadership is generalized to a group as opposed to a specific person, there is greater potential for an appropriate division of labor, decision making power, and responsibility within the project, as well as diversity in thought and ideas*. This will broaden the spectrum of contributors to the leadership effort, enhancing the opportunity for success. This is not to say, however, that a project led by a charismatic individual is doomed to failure.

SUSTAINING YOUR VISION

The Manchester Craftsman's Guild

Pittsburgh, Pennsylvania

A center for inner-city, public school students that teaches life skills and provides rigorous training to entice them off the streets and into school.

The Manchester Craftsman's Guild (MCG), one of the foremost cultural community programs in the nation, was founded in Pittsburgh in 1968 to provide free arts training to children and senior citizens. Four years into the program, Bill Strickland, director of Pittsburgh's Bidwell Training Center, an anti-poverty program providing vocational training for minority students and single mothers, was asked to be executive director for both posts. Strickland agreed and, taking his vision of training people in life skills, fueled by the pivotal role that a ceramics teacher had played in his own development, moved both organizations into the forefront of the community development field.

Since the early 1970s, the Bidwell Training Center has expanded to offer programs in information sciences, culinary arts, pharmacy, and medically related fields to Eastern European ex-steel workers, as well as its traditional clientele. MCG has evolved into an educational program that provides discipline and rigorous training in the arts to inner-city, public school students. MCG also stresses parental involvement in their children's educational experiences and offers adult continuing education courses. The goal of the program is to entice young people to staying off the streets and in school. Or, in Strickland's words, "we're about saving kids." Many MCG students who had no previous thought of attending college end up being the first in their families to do so.

Strickland has secured huge funding grants from foundations like the Heinz Endowment and Mellon Bank and built a $9 million, 62,000 square-foot building that houses a 350-seat auditorium, a gallery, a 200-seat restaurant, and classroom space, as well as state-of-the-art equipment. He has also been instrumental in designing and implementing training programs for leadership and the integration of cultural strategies into the work of community development corporations.

If you ask the staff about the organization's vitality, they explain that MCG is Bill Strickland and Bill Strickland is MCG. But they are quick to explain that he is not the driving force behind the individual programs. The project directors are people who were drawn to MCG by Strickland's energy and who resonated with his vision. Once they gained positions at the Guild, they were given a great deal of creative flexibility in developing and expanding their own projects, so that each carries the distinctive stamp of that person. This has inspired great devotion; they, too, have become synonymous with their vision and their programs and are the lifeblood of the Guild. By cultivating leadership on all levels, Strickland has ensured the vitality and durability of his project.

CONTINUE BUILDING SUPPORT

In addition to building strong internal mechanisms, one way to make sure that a project can succeed in the field is to cultivate support from the larger community. There are a number of strategies for bringing attention to and increasing understanding about a program.

For example, an organization that is strongly linked to other groups and funding sources can become an important ally. Take time to introduce someone from a pivotal organization to your program and describe its value, both to the community and to that organization. One-on-one conversations are particularly helpful in drawing well-connected support because they make the program seem more real, and they provide an opportunity to ask questions. *A dedicated ally within a pivotal organization can help bring attention and more substantive support to your program.*

Attention can also be built from the bottom up by keeping people informed about the project. Newsletters, easily produced using a computer, help introduce programs to new audiences and keep organizations in touch with a wide range of people. Local networks can also be expanded by gaining coverage in the local media. By issuing press releases at events and inviting reporters to attend them, considerable media attention can be drawn to the project.

When developing a theme for publicity, keep it simple — the message should be concise, clear, and easy to remember. Run documents in front of someone who is unfamiliar with the topic to make sure that it does not use jargon or assume knowledge that will be unfamiliar to a most people. In both cases, remember that many people are used to reading and processing information in sound bites. Short, easily digestible components reach the widest audience. This does not mean that a document cannot go into depth, particularly in newsletters. Instead, large blocks of text should be broken up with quotes, boxes, and subheads.

Seeking out places where people gather information outside the traditional media is another way to widen the base of support for the project. Post information at community bulletin boards, in neighborhood presses, in religious facilities, and on cable access channels. As more people turn to the Internet, posting information on a directory like PeaceNet can advertise your partnership or program to like-minded individuals, projects, and resources all over the world.

One of the best ways to convince people of a program's effectiveness, however, is to have them participate in it. Culture, when used in community problem solving, is by nature experiential. Those who see culture as a frill can best come to understand the profound manner in which a cultural experience shapes people by sharing in that same experience.

Many of the factors that shape implementation are specific to local circumstances and project parameters. Resources for carrying out particular approaches and for coping with snarls abound; many of them are listed in **Appendices A and B**. But by now, using this book, you or your organization should have the basic tools needed to develop and put a project in place.

MARKING THE BEGINNING

CHAPTER FIVE

CONCLUSION

In the struggle to balance city budgets or to keep young people in school and out of trouble, turning to the topic of cultural resources can seem frivolous. However, in city after city around the country, people are increasingly aware that cultural resources can be more than children's pictures drawn in crayon or artwork hung in museums. With this understanding that culture, rather than being a frill, is truly an integral component to a healthy society, comes a more complex approach of community problem solving.

Cultural partnerships, built with the community or with those approaching social problems from different perspectives, offer an incisive ground-breaking and foundation-laying tool for today's devastating social ailments. As these past chapters have demonstrated, cultural processes work for a number of reasons.

Cultural resources give individuals the opportunity to encounter success in a setting that is fun — an experience that can build self-esteem and enhance the sense of possibility. They train people in such basic life skills as discipline and decision making, as well as creative and critical thinking — skills that are necessary for success in the information age. They offer an avenue for communication that is safer than confrontation or direct statements. And they help put people in proximity to others who can identify or address that individual's or community's needs.

Cultural resources are also effective on a larger, community level. They provide an effective way to transmit information about culture and ethnicity in a nonthreatening manner, making them a powerful instrument for addressing racial issues. They also are useful in restoring a sense of identity to a community. Furthermore, cultural resources help build a sense of communitywide unity that can extend beyond ethnicity, particularly for regions where the sense of identity and rootedness in community has eroded.

Successful cultural community collaborations are based on four essential factors.

1) All parties must have a clear sense of what they are seeking to do together and how it is beneficial to each. Because the community problem solving process takes time, it is important that the partners stay interested and involved for the long haul.

2) A well-defined relationship, based on open communication, is crucial. This rule applies to both the project partners and the targeted community. When it comes down to sharing an idea, working through a problem, or asking for assistance on a project, it is the people who we know and trust that we will go to first. As long as this sense exists between the parties, they are more likely to work through difficulties and stretch for new ground.

3) The partners must have the skills to equitably negotiate their work. Bridging different working styles, realms of expertise, and relationship to the larger community requires that roles be clearly defined and well balanced. Organizations that understand and approve of the terms of their work are less likely to feel threatened by or dissatisfied with their partners.

4) The partners must never cease planning; they must always be reviewing goals, action plans, and programs to reassess what is being done and why it is happening. They must be prepared to make changes when they become necessary, continue building support, and start anew when the process comes to a close.

The specific community problem solving process is ultimately different for each set of partners and every constellation of concerns. But the key to meeting pressing needs in a time of shrinking resources is structured, applied creativity. Studying what has succeeded before and projecting dreams into the future offers guidance for how to make best use of the present. Creative process, through trial and error, allows people to put together new combinations of resources and arrive at unique answers. Whatever the materials, colors, or media you and your partners choose, by engaging in this arena you are already on your way to innovative solutions.

APPENDIX A
PARTNERS FOR LIVABLE COMMUNITIES:
A PARTNER IN ACTION

Partners for Livable Communities, with nearly twenty years of experience in facilitating community partnerships, is a powerful resource for making the process of building cultural community collaborations easier. Along with this book, Partner's larger "Culture Builds Communities" campaign offers extensive research, conferences, and technical assistance that can benefit both institutions and communities.

Throughout Partners' work, we have found that small steps can lead to the realization of big ideas and that cultural resources can be successfully recruited to tackle our society's most pressing social and economic needs. Some highlights of Partners' projects include

■ investigating the innovative role that parks can play in addressing the needs of youth at risk for the Ford Foundation, with findings detailed in a manual directed toward parks and recreation departments

■ with the support of a grant from the Rockefeller Foundation, researching how individual artists and art managers create change in the larger community, including why cultural strategies are not used more often and how to facilitate social action leadership in the cultural sector

■ convening a national leadership forum at the Smithsonian Institution that drew 170 geographically and professionally diverse community leaders to explore how to improve community problem solving by utilizing cultural resources

■ instigating partnerships between museums and community-based organizations to build civic pride, better understanding of peoples and cultures, and expand community involvement in museums, with the American Association of Museums

■ developing fifteen long-term collaborative cultural projects between thirty-two New York metropolitan area community development corporations and cultural organizations, in conjunction with Citibank

Partners offers a number of frameworks for teaching the effective marshaling of cultural resources for social agendas.

STRATEGIC CONSULTING ON COLLABORATIVE PARTNERSHIPS

Raising the Issues Partners will convene community stakeholders in a day-long session to strategize on how to address a self-identified pressing local concern. After hearing a presentation from an expert in this area, the day will be spent working in small groups to identify possible cultural strategies and to lay the groundwork for future coalition building.

Strategic Planning This six-month project focuses on visioning, goal setting, and the actual process of achieving a cultural collaboration to address social issues. Through workshops, surveys, and individual consultations, Partners will foster partnerships among a wide range of participants and enable them to devise an implementation and funding strategy.

The Cultural Compact Partners also offers a more complex, one- to two-year process that encompasses both planning and implementation. Above and beyond visioning and planning, this option includes assistance in institutionalizing a collaborative cultural strategy to ensure long-term stability and continuity.

MAKING YOUR INSTITUTION A FULCRUM OF CHANGE

Partners offers strategic advice on how to reposition traditional cultural institutions as community stakeholders. Based on our work in laboratory cities around the country, Partners has found that institutions like museums, libraries, parks departments, and zoos can broaden their base of support and reinvigorate their missions by expanding their vision and reformatting their programming.

CREATING SAFETY NETS FOR YOUTH

Given the emerging crisis of youth at risk, and the importance of creating programs to meet the needs of these youth after school, on weekends, and during the summers, Partners intends to create diverse, citywide cultural collaborations that forge new partnerships with those resources already in place.

INFORMATION SHARING

During its research and pilot project work, Partners discovered programs all across the United States that are successfully creating positive changes in their communities by using cultural resources. However, we found that few people are aware of the contributions such projects can make. Therefore, Partners disseminates information on successful cultural collaborations through reports, booklets, regional conferences, and awards.

APPENDIX B
FURTHER RESOURCES FOR CULTURAL COMMUNITY COLLABORATIONS

ASSESSMENT

Co-Arts Assessment Handbook
Jessica Davis, Harvard Project Zero, Harvard University, Cambridge, MA

Based on four years of field work, this self-assessment handbook provides a framework for appraising community art centers that focus on the education in economically disadvantaged communities.

(see also EDUCATION and THE ROLE OF CULTURAL RESOURCES)

New Approaches to Evaluating Community Initiatives
James P. Connell, et. al.,
The Aspen Institute, Washington, DC

This 225-page publication discusses some of the challenges facing designers, funders, managers, and evaluators of comprehensive community initiatives, particularly problems associated with design, implementation, or evaluation of innovative, cross-discipline anti-poverty programs. Through a series of essays by a wide range of experts, it provides many suggestions for how to overcome evaluation problems and to develop new models.

COMMUNITY BUILDING

Building the Collaborative Community: Mobilizing Citizens for Action
Eva Schindler-Rainman and Ronald Lippitt, University of California Extension, Riverside, CA

This 164-page book offers practical and tested strategies for rebuilding collaborative communities. Based on work in 88 communities, the authors offer a variety of adaptable successful tools, procedures, and resources and warn of troublesome issues.

Building the Community from the Inside Out: a Path Toward Finding and Mobilizing a Community's Assets
John McKnight, ACTA Publications, Chicago, IL

A guide for "asset-based community development," summarizing lessons learned by studying hundreds of successful community building initiatives. Using plain terms, the book spells out how communities can rediscover and map their assets, how local strengths can be combined and mobilized to build a more self-reliant community, and how government and grant-givers can contribute to this process.

Consensus Organizing: Concept and Background Paper
Michael Eichler, Local Initiatives Support Corporation, New York, NY

A description of "consensus organizing," a process of building community development corporations (CDCs) through combining grassroots leadership with the resources of the business community. Outlines the formation of sixteen CDCs that use coalition-style community problem solving rather than an adversarial approach.

The State of the American Community: Empowerment for Local Action
Partners for Livable Communities, Washington, DC

This book provides both a theoretical and a practical report of Partners' Shaping Growth in American Communities program — a five-year study in seventy-two communities on what defines livable places. Special essays by national experts provide thought-provoking commentary on leadership, empowerment, regional thinking, and financial trends, backed by more than 100 best practices of community action.

COMMUNITY PARTICIPATION

Community Visioning: Citizen Participation in Strategic Planning
International City/County Management Association, Washington, DC

This fifteen-page report discusses how local government can get a wide range of citizens involved in planning the future of their community. Six case studies explore various approaches for achieving diversity, helping citizens develop informed recommendations, and testing public opinion.

A Guide to Community Visioning: A Hands-On Information Guide for Local Communities
Oregon Visions Project, Portland, OR

A hands-on community organizing manual that provides case studies from various cities in Oregon, showing how visioning, community empowerment, and strategic planning lead to action.

A New Way of Listening
Institute for Development of Educational Activities, Inc., Dayton, OH

A seventeen-minute video tape discussing the value of focus group interviews. Includes a taped example of a focus group of community constituents under the direction of a skilled moderator.

CONFLICT RESOLUTION AND MANAGEMENT SKILLS

Getting to Yes
Rodger Fisher and Bill Ury, Penguin Publishers, New York, NY

Considered a classic in conflict resolution, this 200-page book offers a step-by-step strategy for coming to mutually acceptable agreements in conflict situations.

Getting Together
Rodger Fisher and Scott Brown, Penguin Publishers, New York, NY

The sequel to *Getting to Yes*, this 216-page book offers a straightforward approach to creating relationships that can deal with difficulties as they arise, including initiating, negotiating, and sustaining partnerships.

How to Make Meetings Work
Michael Doyle and David Strauss, Jove, Berkeley Publishing, New York, NY

A practical guide to running meetings that encourage full group participation, including how to draw up agendas, finding meeting rooms, and determining seating arrangements.

APPENDIX B

Program for Community Problem Solving
Washington Office of the National Civic League
915 15th Street NW, Suite 601
Washington, DC 20005
202/783-2961

This organization helps community leaders develop collaborative decision making tools through training and technical assistance in process, program design, facilitation, and mediation. PCPS also offers hands-on guides on many aspects of collaborative making and conflict resolution.

Resolving Conflict: Strategies for Local Government
Margaret S. Herrman, International City/County Management Association, Washington, DC

Practical advice and techniques on how to deal within and outside your organization on issues such as how to identify and resolve cultural conflict, how to facilitate consensus, and how to match your leadership style to the type of conflict. This 232-page book also explores public participation and strategies for long-term success.

Study Circles Resource Center
P.O. Box 203
Pomfret, CT 06258
860/928-2616

This nonprofit organization seeks to advance deliberative democracy and raise the quality of public life through small group, participatory, democratic discussions. Designed to strengthen community connections and solve problems, this process is spelled out through issue guides and how-to publications, as well as direct assistance.

CULTURAL INSTITUTIONS

Museums in the Life of the City: Final Report 1989-1992
The Philadelphia Initiative for Cultural Pluralism, Partners for Livable Communities, Washington, DC

This forty-eight-page booklet shows how museums can play a larger role in the social fabric of the community. It focuses on eleven pilot projects in Philadelphia, highlighting the potential for partnerships between museums and the cities they serve. The findings are applicable to every American city and town working toward increased multicultural understanding and improved community standards.

Museums in the Life of the City: Strategies for Community Partnerships
The Philadelphia Initiative for Cultural Pluralism, American Association of Museums, Washington, DC

Intended to help museums begin the necessary steps to build bridges toward fuller realization of their public service role, this forty-seven-page booklet outlines the process that museums and community partners went through in the Museums in the Life of the City pilot projects.

Wild Kingdoms in the City
Partners for Livable Communities and Karlsberger Companies, Washington, DC

This seventy-six page volume, the proceedings of Partners' 1992 Wild Kingdoms in the City conference, shows how aquariums, zoos, and botanical gardens contribute to communities in ways that go beyond the obvious linking of people with nature. The stories told in this book document the ways in which these "wild kingdoms" bolster local economies, serve community residents, and enhance community images.

(see also YOUTH)

ECONOMICS

Art Space and Economic Development Experience in Six Cities
Partners for Livable Places for the Office of Business and Economic Development of the District of Columbia, Washington, DC

A 230-page report that reviews arts districts and major mixed-use development in six U.S. cities. Each case study documents the public-private partnership arrangements for arts spaces in the cities of Dallas, San Diego, San Francisco, Winston-Salem, St. Paul-Minneapolis, and Cleveland.

The Economics of Amenity: Community Futures and the Quality of Life
Robert H. McNulty, R. Leo Penne, and Dorothy R. Jacobson, Partners for Livable Places, Washington, DC

Drawing upon the experience of cities throughout North America, this 156-page book describes how communities are using their livability — downtowns, performing arts, history, culture, and civic pride — to stimulate business investments, develop tourism, and increase and retain economic growth.

Jobs, the Arts, and the Economy
National Assembly of Local Arts Agencies, Washington, DC

This nineteen-page pamphlet highlights findings from NALAA's "Arts in Economy" study, a three-year, 33-community economic impact study of the nonprofit arts industry. In addition, it features the salient findings of related economic impact studies, making the case that arts is an industry that supports jobs, provides personal income, and generates significant revenue to the local, state, and federal government.

Making the Connection: Economic Development, Workforce Development, and Urban Poverty
Joseph Stillman, The Conservation Company, New York, NY

This study presents examples of work being done around the country to address urban poverty through a combination of workforce and economic development investments. The book reveals diverse approaches to the task, basic elements of successful programs, and lessons for action.

EDUCATION

The Arts and Education: Partners in Achieving Our National Education Goals
Goals 2000 Arts Education Partnership, Washington, DC

A thirty-two-page report and companion brochure outlining how the arts can help achieve each of the eight National Education Goals and articulating why the arts must be central to successful education reform efforts. The publication also identifies a number of critical actions that must happen at the state and community levels for full realization of the benefits the arts can bring to education.

Beyond Creating: The Place for Art in America's Schools
The Getty Center for Education in the Arts, Santa Monica, CA

"Beyond Creating" introduces the reader to a new concept for teaching art in America's schools that is gaining acceptance in art and educational communities across the country. Seven case studies, of selected school districts approaching art education as fundamental to a child's learning, support the assumption that art is basic to education. Seventy-seven-pages.

Harvard Project Zero and Project Co-Arts
Harvard Graduate School of Education
Room 321, Longfellow Hall
Appian Way
Cambridge, MA 02138
617/495-4342

Project Zero is a program documenting the role of the arts in education through the theory of multiple intelligences. The project director, Howard Gardener, has written a number of books in this area.

Project Co-Arts has conducted studies of specific approaches such as community art centers that focus on education in economically disadvantaged areas.

(see also ASSESSMENT and THE ROLE OF CULTURAL RESOURCES)

Intersections: Community Arts and Education Collaborations
Craig Dreeszen, et. al., Arts Extension Service, University of Massachusetts, Amherst, MA

Based on a report done for the National Endowment for the Arts, this forty-six-page book documents community arts and education partnerships and examines what contributes to and what blocks successful community and school partnerships on behalf of arts in education.

National Arts Education Research Center
New York University
32 Washington Place
New York, NY 10003
212/998-5050

Copies of reports on the impact of the arts on education can be obtained through the Office of Education at New York University.

FUNDING

The Art of Asking: How to Solicit Philanthropic Gifts
Paul H. Schneiter, Fund-Raising Institute, Ambler, PA

This 176-page book explores the full scope of fundraising, including: eight key motivations for giving; what must happen before you ask for a gift; and four asking techniques. Case studies, interviews with individual donors, and extensive comments from the author's own experience show how these strategies can be put into action.

Artist in Business: Basic Business Practices
Craig Dreeszen, Arts Extension Services, University of Massachusetts, Amherst, MA

This 118-page booklet helps artists manage their careers and set priorities in areas like business operations, record-keeping, taxes, the budget process, legal rights, and financial resources.

Corporate Community Involvement
The President's Task Force on Private Sector Initiatives, Partners for Livable Communities, Washington, D.C.

This thirty-one-page booklet provides an overview of the strategies utilized by

APPENDIX B

corporations to respond to community needs and explores the methods companies seek to establish relationships with community groups and government.

Don't Just Applaud, Send Money: The Most Successful Strategies for Funding and Marketing the Arts
Alvin H. Reiss, Theatre Communications Group, New York, NY

Over 100 case studies, many illustrated with examples of the actual materials, showing how arts groups developed unique promotions and funding tactics.

Enterprise in the Nonprofit Sector
James C. Crimmins and Mary Keil, Partners for Livable Places and the Rockefeller Brothers Fund, Washington, DC

This 144-page publication looks at the issues, benefits, and risks involved when nonprofit organizations supplement traditional funding sources with entrepreneurial activities. Based on surveys and interviews, this report focuses on case studies of eleven enterprising organizations.

Funding for Museums, Archives, and Special Collections
Denise Wallen and Karen Cantrell, Oryx Press, Phoenix, AZ

This 355-page directory was designed to facilitate the search for financial support for cultural institutions from aquariums, to natural history museums to historical archives. Over 500 listings tap into private and corporate foundations, direct giving, government, association, and professional sources.

Resource Development Handbook: Untapped Public Funding for the Arts
Ed. Dian Magie, National Assembly of Local Arts Agencies, Washington, DC

This 148-page handbook provides examples of a variety of funding mechanisms that local arts agencies are tapping in large urban areas, medium cities, and small towns. Using the framework of this book, readers should be able to identify several examples that can be replicated in their communities.

THE ROLE OF CULTURAL RESOURCES

Art in Other Places: Artists at Work in America's Community and Social Institutions
William Cleveland, Praeger Publishers, Westport, CT

This book chronicles the work of twenty-two writers, performers, and visual artists who have pioneered arts programs in community and social institutions in the U.S. over the past twenty years. It includes case studies, research, and descriptions of the wide variety of artistic, educational, and therapeutic approaches used in each case. It also recounts many of the financial and political strategies employed to build and sustain support for these endeavors.

Crossroads: Reflections on the Politics of Culture
Don Adams and Arlene Goldbard, DNA Press, Ukiah, CA

A fresh look at the politics of culture and cultural democracy in the U.S. This book will help artists, educators, and organizers decipher the cultural impact of U.S. history, explore the social meanings of the arts, and discover the essential links between art and democratic competence.

APPENDIX B

Culture and Communities: The Arts in the Life of American Cities
Robert H. McNulty, Patricia C. Jones, and Laura R. Green, Partners for Livable Communities, Washington, DC

This thirty-one-page report, based on more than twenty case studies from sites across the country, presents an in-depth analysis of the role that arts institutions play in the life of cities and shows that the arts can be used as an essential factor in determining how we enjoy and appreciate our own communities.

Games for Actors and Non-Actors
Augusto Boal, Routledge, New York, NY

Boal — a Brazilian theater director, writer, and theorist — has developed a body of theatrical techniques based, in part, on Paulo Friere's education for liberation. This practical guide describes how his methods can transform theater into a democratic arena where the spectator becomes "spect-actor."

Generating Community: Intergenerational Partnerships Through the Expressive Arts
Susan Perlstein, Elders Share the Arts, New York, NY

This sixty-four-page book is a guide and resource for people who wish to create and implement intergenerational arts programs, including approaches to agency partnerships, icebreakers, public presentations, curricula, issues to watch for, and troubleshooting solutions.

Mapping the Terrain: New Genre Public Art
Ed. Suzanne Lacy, Bay Press, Seattle, WA

Featuring essays by well-known artist activists like Judith Baca and Mary Jean Jacob, this 293-page book explores both conceptual frameworks and activist strategies for using art resources to explore race, gender, sexuality, ecology, and urbanization.

Reimaging America: The Arts of Social Change
Eds. Mark O'Brien & Craig Little, New Society Publishers, Philadelphia, PA

A rare forum for politically active artists to discuss how they make, present, and evaluate their work. Over fifty contributors explore how the choices they make relate to issues such as the impact of the arts on social movements, the politics of process, the relationship between artists and their communities, and the growing influence of the mass media.

Safe Havens: Portraits of Education Effectiveness in Community Art Centers that Focus on Education in Economically Disadvantaged Communities
Jessica Davis, et.al., Harvard Project Zero, Harvard University, Cambridge, MA

Five in-depth portraits of exemplary veteran community art centers that focus on education in economically disadvantaged communities, along with an analysis of their effectiveness according to the Co-Arts assessment plan.

(see also ASSESSMENT and EDUCATION)

APPENDIX B

TERMS

Dictionary of CED Terms: A Resource Book for Practitioners and Funders
California Community Economic Development Association, Oakland, CA

Intended to facilitate common ground by providing definitions of acronyms and terms used in community-based development programs. Also includes listings of federal programs used by CDCs and relevant national nonprofit organizations. 155 pages.

YOUTH

Best Practices for Building a Caring Community: Delivering Social Services to Youth at Risk Through Urban Park and Recreation Programs
Partners for Livable Communities, Washington, DC

The more than twenty best practices presented in this booklet show how sports, outdoor education, and other recreational programs can provide a higher quality of life for urban youth. Forty pages.

Bridging the Gap: A Rationale for Enhancing the Role of Community Organizations in Promoting Youth Development
Karen J. Pittman with Marlene Wright, Center for Youth Development at the Academy for Educational Development, Washington, DC

A working paper that offers a working definition of youth development based on existing theories and discussions, and an argument for strengthening the role of the nonschool voluntary sector in promoting youth development. One of three commissioned papers on this topic.

A Matter of Time: Risk and Opportunity in the Out-of-School Hours (Abridged Version)
Carnegie Council on Adolescent Development, New York, NY

A forty-page booklet covering the findings of the Carnegie Council on Adolescent Development. In addition to providing facts and figures, it discusses how community organizations can support youth development, how to strengthen community programs for youth, and resources for after school programs.

Part of the Solution: Creative Alternatives for Youth
National Assembly of State Arts Agencies, Washington, DC

Eleven case studies of programs that use culture to meet the needs of youth in creative ways. Its ninety-six pages also include brief descriptions of projects launched by fifty-six state and regional arts organizations.

The State of America's Children Yearbook, 1995
Children's Defense Fund, Washington, DC

Using statistics, trends, overviews, and recommendations, this 136-page volume covers a wide range of issues affecting youth. Chapters focus on the federal climate, family income, health, child care and early childhood development, hunger and nutrition, violence, housing and homelessness, children and families in crisis, teen pregnancy and youth development, and education.

APPENDIX B

INDEX OF BEST PRACTICES

NAME AND ADDRESS	PAGE

Artists Collective   ii, 62, 63
35 Clark Street
Hartford, CT 06120
203/527-3205
A community-focused performing arts center, strengthening knowledge of African-American heritage and building life skills through performances and classes.

Arts in the Basic Curriculum   ii, 9
Project/Target 2000 Arts in Education Grant Program
South Carolina Arts Commission
1800 Gervais Street
Columbia, SC 29201
803/734-8696
A school reform package including curriculum frameworks, funding, and public relations to boost perception of arts as essential to education.

Artspace Projects, Inc.   ii, 65
250 Third Avenue North
Suite 111
Minneapolis, MN 55401
612/339-4372
A nonprofit real estate developer, working to create physical space for the production of art within a community setting.

Baltimore City   ii, 52, 53
Life Museums
800 East Lombard Street
Baltimore, MD 21202
410/396-8394
An urban history museum, consisting of eight historic landmarks in three inner-city sites, deeply involved in neighborhood revitalization.

Bend in the River   ii, 10, 11
c/o Penny Gronen
Public Information Officer
50 West 13th Street
Dubuque, IA 52001
319/589-4116
A festival to address racism, including both diversity training and multicultural food, music, and art exchanges.

Black Economic Union   ii, 34, 35
of Greater Kansas City
1601 E. 18th Street, Suite 300
Kansas City, MO 64108
816/474-1080
A community development corporation that is restoring a traditional Black neighborhood as a historic district through creating both housing and cultural events.

Break the Cycle Teen   ii, 7, 8
Theatre Troupe
City of Longmont
1050 Lashley Street
Longmont, CO 80501
303/651-8580
Troubled youth perform self-written plays and provide peer counseling for other youth on critical issues.

Brooklyn In Touch   ii, 48, 53, 61
Information Center, Inc.
One Hanson Place, Room 2504
Brooklyn, NY 11243
718/230-3200
An organization that provides management assistance to nonprofit organizations. Conducts technical assistance on process considerations for the Citibank grant program.

Bronx Council on the Arts ii, 48
1738 Hone Avenue
New York, NY 10461
718/931-9500
An organization that increases awareness of and participation in the arts and nurtures the professional development of artists and arts organizations. Conducts technical assistance for the Citibank grant program.

Cheyenne Botanic Garden ii
700 S. Lions Drive
Cheyenne, WY 82001
307/637-6458
A public garden staffed by at-risk youth, disabled, and elderly volunteers that provides vegetables for food shelves and plants for city green spaces.

City Lights Program ii, 11, 12
Humanities Council of Washington, D.C.
1331 H Street NW, Suite 902
Washington, DC 20005
202/347-1732
A cultural history project that brings storytellers and artists from various ethnic traditions into public housing and provides funds for heritage projects.

Colfax Cultural Center Complex
see South Bend Heritage Foundation

Community Agency for 49, 63
Senior Citizens
56 Bay Street
Staten Island, NY 10301
718/981-6226
An organization that creates and maintains community-based social and health support services for adults over age sixty, so that they may lead viable, independent lives.

Council on the Arts ii, 49, 63
and Humanities for Staten Island
1000 Richmond Terrace
Staten Island, NY 10301
718/447-3329
An organization that develops, fosters, and promotes the arts and cultural activities; disseminates cultural information; and serves as a conduit for outreach programs for both arts programs and the general public.

Cultural Arts Program ii
City of Dayton, Ohio
101 West Third Street
Dayton, OH 45402
513/443-3691
Coordinates a range of community arts programs including festivals, capital improvement partnerships, training programs for both youth and adults in art leadership, promoting local cultural institutions and facilitating their outreach efforts, and cataloging cultural resources.

Cultural Collaborative Jamaica ii, 54, 55
90-04 161st Street
Jamaica, NY 11432
718/291-0282
Eight cultural organizations, two businesses, one university, and one development company that work together to create programs that use cultural resources to address community issues.

Def Dance Jam Workshop
see Downtown Art Co.

Downtown Art Co. ii, 57, 58
280 Broadway, Room 412
New York, NY 10007
212/732-1201
A nonprofit arts organization developing projects which bring professional artists into community contexts to create dance, theater, and music projects with teens, families in shelters, and single mothers.

Forsyth County Library   i, 26
660 West 5th Street
Winston-Salem, NC 27101
910/727-2556
Library that undertook a community visioning process to ensure it will be a welcoming resource and community focal point.

Gowanus Arts Exchange   ii, 30, 31
295 Douglass Street
Brooklyn, NY 11217
718/596-5250
An organization that promotes the performing arts and arts education, serves as a neighborhood home for artists and their audiences, and acts as an advocate for cultural diversity and inventiveness.

The Guadalupe Cultural   ii, 13
Arts Center
1300 Guadalupe Street
San Antonio, TX 78207
210/271-3151
The foremost Latino multidisciplinary cultural center in the country, providing a host of programs in a wide range of media and promoting economic development among the Latino population.

Humanities Council of
Washington, DC
see City Lights Program

Learning Through Education   ii
and Arts Partnerships
c/o the Center for Creative Education
3359 Belvedere Road, Suite S
West Palm Beach, FL 33406
407/687-5200
An arts integration program working in schools and with a range of cultural and community organizations after school to provide a seamless web of education and services for young people.

The Living Stage   ii, 64
Theatre Company
6th & Maine Avenue SW
Washington, DC 20024
202/554-9066
An improvisational theater program helping emotional disturbed, physically disabled, and at-risk youth.

Manchester Craftsman's Guild   ii, 68
1815 Metropolitan
Pittsburgh, PA 15233
412/323-4000
A center for inner-city, public school students that teaches life skills and provides rigorous art training to entice them into staying off the streets and in school.

Mill Tapestry Project   ii
Richards Free Library
58 North Main Street
Newport, NH 03773
603/863-3430
A tapestry telling the story of life in a New Hampshire textile mill town, paired with educational and cultural programs that engage the community in critical examination of the area's industrial heritage.

Museums in the Life of the City   ii
c/o Portia Hamilton-Sperr
The Philadelphia Initiative for Cultural Pluralism
2038 Spruce Street
Philadelphia, PA 19103
215/732-2038
A project assisting in partnership building between museums and ethnic organizations to facilitate better understanding between the two parties.

INDEX

Neighborhood Housing   ii, 30, 31
Services
121 West 27th Street, 4th floor
New York, NY 10001
212/645-6363
A not-for-profit organization working to increase investment in declining neighborhoods, to encourage and support neighborhood self-reliance, and to create, preserve, and promote affordable housing.

New York Main   i, 49, 63
Street Alliance
35 West Main Street
Mt. Kisco, NY 10549
718/981-7816
A statewide organization dedicated to maintaining the vibrancy of New York's historic commercial corridors. Works with local development corporations to benefit businesses and residents.

Northwestern University   ii
Settlement Association
1400 Augusta Boulevard
Chicago, IL 60622
312/278-7471
A social service agency providing services ranging from food shelves to video, dance, and drumming programs. Currently renovating a theater to create a community arts center.

Phoenix Parks, Recreation   ii, 14
and Library Department
City of Phoenix
2705 North 15th Avenue
Phoenix, AZ 85007
602/262-7371
A recreation program offering employment, life, and remedial skills to youth at risk in community centers, from mobile recreation units, and in partnership with other organizations.

Portsmouth Community   ii, 15, 16, 43
Development Group
440 High Street, Suite 204
Portsmouth, VA 23704
804/399-0925
A community development corporation that created a Caribbean music program to teach youth life skills and is generating spaces for the arts through rehabilitating buildings.

Project for Public Spaces   ii
153 Waverly Place
New York, NY 10014
212/620-5660
Experts on the design and management of public space and how it is used. Involved in implementing the "Public Libraries in Partnership with Community" program, along with Partners for Livable Communities.

Project Self Discovery   ii, 66, 67
899 Logan Street, Suite 207
Denver, CO 80203
303/830-8500
An arts-focused program to help drug-addicted youths remain off drugs.

Race to Knowledge   ii
5134 South Michigan Avenue
Chicago, IL 60615
312/905-1647
An after-school educational program to raise self-esteem, provide health education, and teach academic skills through computer science, science and math, and the performing arts.

Sangre Latina   ii, 59
P.O. Box 2907
Richmond, CA 94801-9991
510/839-7117
A theater program for at-risk Latino youth to further their commitment to higher education.

INDEX

Social and Public Art   i
Resource Center
685 Venice Boulevard
Venice, CA 90291
310/822-9560
A multicultural arts center that produces, exhibits, distributes, and preserves public art works, particularly murals.

South Bend Heritage Foundation   ii, 1, 2
914 Lincoln Way West
South Bend, IN 46616
219/289-1066
A community development corporation offering community organizing training and housing and commercial development services. Also the developer and manager of the Colfax Cultural Center Complex, a space for educational, artistic, and social service agencies.

Three Rivers Arts Festival   ii, 51
207 Sweetbriar Street
Pittsburgh, PA 15211
412/481-7040
An annual arts festival stressing strong community involvement.

Urban Arts Institute   ii
c/o Center for Third World Organizing
1218 East 21st Street
Oakland, CA 94606
510/533-7583 x9
A research and education center fostering community transformation through the arts. Runs a community arts apprenticeship program that helps young artists develop skills that they can apply to social change projects.

Your Voice Theater
see Gowanus Arts Exchange and Neighborhood Housing Services

INDEX